Cambridge Primary

Hodder Cambridge Primary

Science

Learner's Book

Stage 4

Rosemary Feasey

Series editor: Deborah Herridge

HODDER EDUCATION
AN HACHETTE UK COMPANY

Acknowledgements

The Publisher is extremely grateful to the following schools for their comments and feedback during the development of this series:

Avalon Heights World Private School, Ajman

The Oxford School, Dubai

Al Amana Private School, Sharjah

British International School, Ajman

Wesgreen International School, Sharjah

As Seeb International School, Al Khoud

The publisher would like to thank the following for permission to reproduce copyright material.

p.61 All Science Fair Projects, http://www.all-science-fair-projects.com/print_project_1593_38, info@all-science-fair-projects.com

Photo credits

p.7 *t*, **p.54** *t* © C Squared Studios/Photodisc/Getty Images/Moments in Life OS36; **p.7** *c* © Rawpixel/Fotolia; **p.7** *cr* © Cdelacy/Fotolia; **p.7** *cl* © Jojje11/Fotolia; **p.7** *bl* © Ingram Publishing Limited/Ingram Image Library 500-Flowers; **p.7** *br* © Imagestate Media (John Foxx)/Vol 03 Nature & Animals; **p.9** *tl* © Rudmer Zwerver/Shutterstock; **p.9** *tc* © Eric Isselee/Shutterstock; **p.9** *tc* © Kimberly Soper/Fotolia; **p.9** *t* © Eric Isselee/Shutterstock; **p.9** *bl* © Parmoht hongtong/123rf; **p.9** *br* © Aquapix/Shutterstock; **p.10, p.140** Ingram Publishing Limited/Ingram Image Library 500-Education **p.13** © Arekmalang/Fotolia; **p.15** *cl* © Smuki/Fotolia; **p.15** *c, **p.144** *r* © eAlisa/Fotolia; **p.15** *cr* © Martin81/Shutterstock; **p.15** *b* © Jason salmon/123rf; **p.16** *tl* © Jim Wehtje/Photodisc/Getty Images/X-Ray Vision 30; **p.16** *tl, tc, **p.144** *l* © Jim Wehtje/Photodisc/Getty Images/ X-Ray Vision 30; **p.16** *tr* © Ivy Close Images/Alamy Stock Photo; **p.16** *c* © Alessandro Innamorati/123rf; **p.16** *cr* © Radius Images/Alamy Stock Photo; **p.19** © Andegro4ka/123rf; **p.21, p.30, p.61** *(both)*, **p.68** *(both)*, **p.107bl, p.110** *tl*, **p.117** © Hachette UK; **p.24** *cl* © Samuel Jolly/123rf; **p.24** *cr* © TMAX/Fotolia; **p.25** © De Visu/Shutterstock; **p.27** © Tim Shepard, Oxford Scientific Films /Getty Images; **p.28** © Thomas Sztanek/123rf; **p.29** *t*, **p.31** *t*, **p.48** *t* © Mauro Rodrigues/ Shutterstock; **p.29** *cl*, **p.141** © Aedka Studio/Shutterstock; **p.29** *cr*, **p.34** *cl* © Imageman/Shutterstock; **p.29** *b* © Domnitsky/Shutterstock; **p.32** © Lady_in_red13/Shutterstock; **p.33** *cl* © Ephotocorp/Alamy Stock Photo; **p.33** *c* © Jehangir Hanafi/Alamy Stock Photo; **p.33** *c* © Simon Reddy/Alamy Stock Photo; **p.33** *cr* © Dinodia Photos /Alamy Stock Photo; **p.34** *cl* © John Kasawa/Shutterstock; **p.34** *c* © Eric Isselee/Shutterstock; **p.34** *c* © Le Do/Shutterstock; **p.34** *cr* © Sattapapan Tratong/123rf; **p.34** *br* © Viennetta/Shutterstock; **p.34** *br* © Viennetta/Shutterstock; **p.35** *cl* © Krasnajasapocka/Fotolia; **p.35** *c* © Thawat Tanhai/123rf; **p.35** *c* © PhotoAlto/Nature 5; **p.35** *cr* © Andreahast/123rf; **p.39** © Gunnar Pippel/Shutterstock; **p.40** © Moreno Soppelsa/Shutterstock; **p.42** *cl* © Stefan Redel/Fotolia; **p.42** *cr* © Mrs Levite/Fotolia; **p.42** *b* © Fluke Samed/Shutterstock; **p.43** © Stan Wayman/Getty Images; **p.44** *t* © Avalon/Photoshot License/Alamy Stock Photo; **p.44** *b* © Joel Nito/Stringer/Getty Images; **p.45** © Heinrich van den Berg/Getty Images; **p.46** © Holbox/Shutterstock; **p.53** © Vera Kuttelvaserova/Fotolia; **p.54** *b* © Charmaine A Harvey/Shutterstock; **p.56** *tl* © Slawomir Zelasko/Shutterstock; **p.56** *tr* © Nevodka/Shutterstock; **p.64** © Lubov Vis/Shutterstock; **p.78** © European Southern Observatory/Science Photo Library; **p.80** © Alchemy/Alamy Stock Photo; **p.83** © PhotosIndia.com LLC/123rf; **p.85** © Trevor Clifford Photography/ Science Photo Library; **p.86** © JTB Media Creation, Inc./Alamy Stock Photo; **p.87** *t* © Paul Glendell/Alamy Stock Photo; **p.87** *b* © Susanna Lee (http://www.tabibito.biz); **p.88** © TFoxFoto/Shutterstock; **p.95** *tl* © Vaclav Mach/Shutterstock; **p.95** *tr* © Maksym Bondarchuk/123FR; **p.95** *tc* © Peter Gudella/Shutterstock; **p.95** *tr* © Petr Malyshev/Shutterstock; **p.95** *tb* © Cobalt/Fotolia; **p.98** © Jimiknightley/iStock/Thinkstock/Getty Images; **p.100** © Sciencephotos /Alamy Stock Photo; **p.107tl** © Damir Khabirov/Shutterstock; **p.107tr** © Penguiin/Shutterstock; **p.107br** © Pelfophoto/Shutterstock; **p.110** *tr* © Ivydale Science & Technology Service; **p.112** © Jose Luis Granados Ortega/EyeEm/Getty Images; **p.115** *tb* © Anan Kaewkhammul/123rf; **p.115** *br* © Eric Isselee/123rf; **p.123** © lOvE lOvE/Shutterstock; **p.125** © DCP Microdevelopments Limited; **p.127** © Dustin Carr & Harold Craighead, Cornell University; **p.128** ©Tom Pavlasek/Shutterstock; **p.129** © Dan Leeth/Alamy Stock Photo; **P.133** © Avalon/Construction Photography/Alamy Stock Photo.

t = top, *b* = bottom, *l* = left, *r* = right, *c* = centre

Practice test exam-style questions are written by the author.

Whilst every effort has been made to carefully check the instructions for practical work described in this book, schools should conduct their own risk assessments in accordance with local health and safety requirements.

Every effort has been made to trace all copyright holders, but if any have been inadvertently overlooked the Publishers will be pleased to make the necessary arrangements at the first opportunity.

Although every effort has been made to ensure that website addresses are correct at time of going to press, Hodder Education cannot be held responsible for the content of any website mentioned in this book. It is sometimes possible to find a relocated web page by typing in the address of the home page for a website, in the URL window of your browser.

Hachette UK's policy is to use papers that are natural, renewable and recyclable products and made from wood grown in sustainable forests. The logging and manufacturing processes are expected to conform to the environmental regulations of the country of origin.

Orders: please contact Bookpoint Ltd, 130 Milton Park, Abingdon, Oxon OX14 4SB. Telephone: (+44) 01235 827720. Fax: (+44) 01235 400454. Lines are open from 9.00–5.00, Monday to Saturday, with a 24-hour message answering service. You can also order through our website: www.hoddereducation.com

© Rosemary Feasey 2017

Published by Hodder Education

A Hachette UK Company

Carmelite House, 50 Victoria Embankment, London EC4Y 0DZ

Impression number   6

Year   2020

Cover illustration © Steve Evans

Illustrations by Vian Oelofsen and Steve Evans

Typeset in FS Albert 15 on 17pt by IO Publishing CC

Printed in Italy

A catalogue record for this title is available from the British Library

9781471884023

Contents

What does a scientist do?

Scientists are people who are interested in the world around them. They ask questions and find the answers by testing their ideas in different ways.

Scientists look for similarities and differences. They sort things into groups so that they can identify, name and classify them. An example is sorting the different animals in the sea.

Scientists compare what happens. An example is putting different objects into water, to find out which objects float or sink.

Scientists make observations using all their senses. They make notes and draw pictures to record what they find out. Scientists keep this information.

Scientists share what they find out about the world. To find information, scientists read books, look on the internet, and watch videos.

Shoe length	Number of people
21 cm	1
24 cm	3
25 cm	3
26 cm	2
27 cm	8
28 cm	5
29 cm	1
30 cm	1
31 cm	1

Scientists test their ideas. They look at the effect that one thing has on another thing in an investigation. Scientists always try to keep the test fair.

Scientific questions must be measurable. Scientists look for that in their results.

How to do a fair test

Scientists think about and do different things in order to carry out a fair test. A fair test is a way to investigate a scientific question. Start at 1 and read the instructions in each box.

(1) Think about what you want to find out. Ask a scientific question. Then investigate, test and measure the results.

(2) What will you do to answer your question? How can you test it?

(3) What equipment will you need to help you? You might need measuring equipment.

(4) Decide which things to change when you do a fair test. What effect will you measure? These are called variables or factors.

(5) Keep your test fair. Change only one variable or factor. Everything else must stay the same.

(6) Observe changes during the fair test. Measure the changes (such as temperature, time or length).

(7) Record your observations (data) to remember what happened. Use a table with two columns to help you. Record what you changed and what you measured.

(8) You could put your data in a chart. This may help you to see the pattern in your results more easily.

(9) The results of your fair test will help you to answer your question. This is the conclusion.

(10) Ask: Was my test a good test? Can I trust my results? How can I improve the test?

(11) Now that you have done your fair test, do you have any new questions? If so, carry out another investigation!

What do you know about life processes?

Think like a scientist!

Think about what you know about living things. All humans and animals do certain things. These things are called **life processes**:

- Living things can **move**.
- Living things can **reproduce** (have young).
- Living things can **grow**.
- Living things need **nutrition** (food and drink).

1

Make a list of five things that change as humans get older.

Talk partners

Talk to your partner and help each other to remember the life processes of humans and animals. Answer these questions.

a What does each life process mean? Give an example of each life process.

b How does a human grow from being a baby to being an adult?

Scientific words

life processes
move
reproduce
grow
nutrition

How do you know it is alive?

1

Look at the photographs. Write a sentence to explain why the thing in each picture is **alive** or **not alive**. The first one has been done for you.

a
chair

The chair is not alive. A chair cannot reproduce, move or grow and does not need nutrition.

b
car

c
shark

d
mobile phone

e
flowering plant

f
lightning

Remember: a thing is alive only if it does the life processes!

Scientific words

alive
not alive

2

What do you do to be a healthy and happy living thing?
Answer each question.

a Which foods do you eat that are healthy for you?

b Which foods can be harmful if you eat too much of them?

c What makes you happy?

d What kind of exercise or sport do you do to stay fit and healthy?

e Draw a picture of yourself. Around the picture, write what you do to stay healthy and happy.

Using your senses

1

Think about what you already know about your senses.

a Draw a picture of yourself to show the five different senses. Label your picture to explain what each sense does and how it helps you.

b When you have finished, find out an amazing fact about one of the senses. Write the fact under your picture.

Scientific words
hearing
sight
taste
touch
smell

2

The five senses are important to humans. Think about them. What are your favourite things and least favourite things to hear (**hearing**), see (**sight**), **taste**, **touch** and **smell**? Copy and complete this table.

Sense	My favourite thing is …	My least favourite thing is …
hearing		
sight		
taste		
touch		
smell		

Talk partners

Talk to your partner. Which sense do you think is the most important? Why? Write down your answer. Then share your ideas with another pair or group.

Did you know?

When you breathe in air, you can smell things. The hairs and mucus inside your nose clean the breathed-in air by trapping dust. This stops the dust moving into your lungs.

Sorting living things into groups

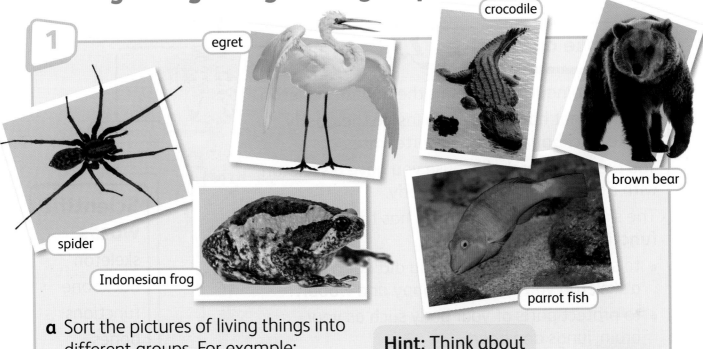

1

egret

crocodile

brown bear

spider

Indonesian frog

parrot fish

a Sort the pictures of living things into different groups. For example:

Has four legs

Eats grass

Lives in water

Hint: Think about how the animal behaves and what it looks like.

b Sort the pictures into **vertebrates** (animals with a backbone) and **invertebrates** (no backbone).

c Use a table like this to sort the vertebrates in the pictures:

Mammal	Bird	Reptile	Fish	Amphibian

Challenge yourself!

Try to sort some of the living things in the pictures into **carnivores** (eat meat), **omnivores** (eat both meat and plants) and **herbivores** (eat plants).

Scientific words

vertebrates

invertebrates

carnivores

omnivores

herbivores

The human skeleton

Think like a scientist!

You are going to learn about the human **skeleton**.

Animals that have a skeleton inside their body with a **backbone** are called vertebrates.

You are a vertebrate because you have a skeleton with a backbone inside your body.

The skeleton is important, and has three main **functions** (jobs). These are:

- to support your body – if you did not have a skeleton you would be floppy and wobbly!
- to protect parts of your body such as your brain, lungs and heart
- to help you move.

backbone

Scientific words

skeleton
backbone
functions
bones
joints

Talk partners

The skeleton is made up of **bones**. What are the names of the different bones? Share your ideas with a partner. How many bones in your own body can you name?

1

You will need...

- large sheet of paper
- pencil

Draw and label a skeleton.

a Ask a partner to lie on the paper. Use the pencil to outline your partner's body.

b Where are the bones in your body? What do they feel and look like? Draw the bones and label them inside the body outline.

Did you know?

The places where our bones meet are called **joints**. Joints are places that allow our bones to move.

2

Where are the joints in your body? Put circles around the joints on your skeleton drawing from Activity 1.

 # Bones

Think like a scientist!

An adult human has 206 bones. This diagram shows the main bones in the human body:

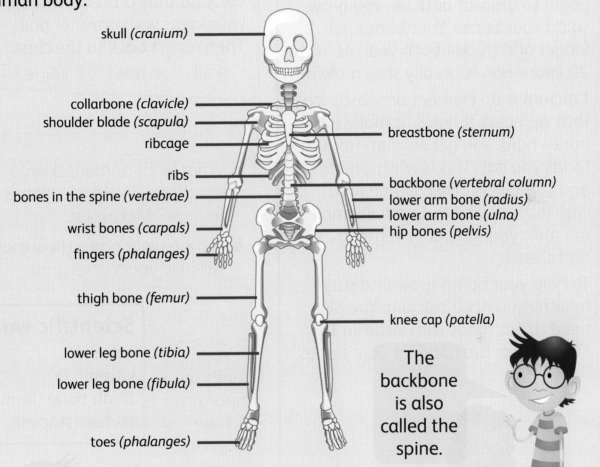

skull (*cranium*)

collarbone (*clavicle*)
shoulder blade (*scapula*)
ribcage

ribs
bones in the spine (*vertebrae*)

wrist bones (*carpals*)
fingers (*phalanges*)

thigh bone (*femur*)

lower leg bone (*tibia*)

lower leg bone (*fibula*)

toes (*phalanges*)

breastbone (*sternum*)

backbone (*vertebral column*)
lower arm bone (*radius*)
lower arm bone (*ulna*)
hip bones (*pelvis*)

knee cap (*patella*)

The backbone is also called the spine.

1

206 bones is a lot!
Did you show that many bones in the skeleton you drew for Activity 1 on page 10? Check your skeleton using the diagram above.
If all the bones above are not on your drawing, add them.

Challenge yourself!

The diagram uses the everyday names of the bones, with the scientific names in brackets.
Can you remember both words?
Ask your partner to test you on both names of each bone.

How the human skeleton grows

Think like a scientist!

Skeletons grow as humans grow. You begin to grow at birth. As you grow, so do your bones. Your bones get longer and thicker each year. At 18 to 20 years, bones usually stop growing.

Calcium is an element or substance that we need. It helps to make our bones hard. You get calcium from the foods you eat. This is why parents and caregivers give children foods with lots of calcium. Some examples are milk, yoghurt, leafy vegetables and cheese.

To help your bones grow and stay healthy you need calcium. You also need to eat foods with **vitamin D**. These foods are good for your bones:

sweet potatoes

cheese · okra

sardines · artichokes · yoghurt · kale

Talk partners

Talk to a partner about the bones below. Which parts of the body do they protect? Discuss your ideas with another pair. Then report back to the class.
- skull
- ribs
- spine

1

a What kinds of foods do you eat that will help your bones to grow? Make a list.

b Draw a plate and a meal that will help your bones grow.

Scientific words

calcium
vitamin D
thigh bone (femur)
stirrup (stapes)

Your bones are important. They support and protect your body.

Did you know?

Your longest bone is your **thigh bone (femur)**. Your smallest bone is the **stirrup (stapes)**, in your ear. It is only about 0.25 cm long.

Your growing bones

> **Talk partners**
>
> Ask a partner: How many more bones does a baby have than an adult? What do you think happens to your bones as you get older?

> A baby has over 300 bones. An adult has 206 bones.

Think like a scientist!

You do not lose bones as you get older, but some bones join together. Therefore, you have fewer bones. As you get older your body grows, and so do the bones inside your body. Your bones become harder and stronger, so that they can support your weight. Strong bones allow you to run, jump, dance and skip!

Babies are not very tall – they are about 46 cm long. A baby's head is about 12 cm long, or about one-quarter of the length of the body.

1

Work with a partner. Measure each other.

a How long is your head? How long (tall) are you from the top of your head to your feet? Copy and complete the table below.

	When I was a baby	Now
length of the head	*12 cm*	
length of the body	*46 cm*	

Challenge yourself!

When you were a baby, your head was one-quarter of the length of your whole body. Is your head still one-quarter of the length of your body? Try to work it out.

What is inside our bones?

Think like a scientist!

Bones are living, and grow as we grow. We have **bone marrow** in the middle of our bones. Bone marrow has a very special job. It makes red and white **blood cells** and sends them to other parts of the body.

Red blood cells carry **oxygen** around the body.

White blood cells are very important because they help to fight illness.

This is a diagram of what a bone looks like.

The **spongy bone** is where the bone grows.

On the outside, the bone is hard

Bone marrow is in the middle of the bone – red and white blood cells are made here.

1

Use any materials you can find to make a model bone, for example, cardboard rolls and sponge. When you have finished, display your model. Make card labels with information next to your bone. Try to use all the scientific words on this page in your labels.

Scientific words

bone marrow

blood cells

oxygen

spongy bone

Human skeleton X-rays

Think like a scientist!

How do we know what bones look like? How do we know if bones are broken? **X-ray** machines take special pictures of the bones in the body. X-rays are used by doctors to look at broken bones. The name for a broken bone is a **fracture**.

1

Look at the X-rays of parts of the human body.

a Match the name of the bone shown on each X-ray using the labels.

b Which X-ray shows a fracture (broken bone)?

i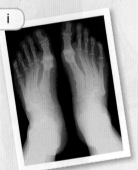

ii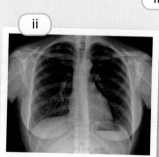

iii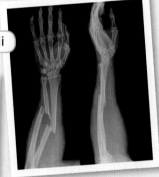

Scientific words
X-ray
fracture
cast

toes (phalanges)

lower arm bones (radius and ulna)

ribcage

Did you know?

Doctors can mend broken bones. To do this, they move the broken parts back together. Then they put on a **cast** to stop the bone from moving. After a certain amount of time the bone heals.

Challenge yourself!

Have you or someone at school broken any bones? Which bones? What happened to cause the bone to break? How will you find out the answers?

Animal skeletons

1

i

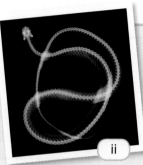

ii

iii

Look at the three X-rays of different animals that are vertebrates.

a Write down the name of each animal.

b Explain how you know which animal is in each X-ray.

Scientific word

exoskeleton

Animals that have a skeleton with a backbone inside their body are called vertebrates.

2

Compare the two skeletons of a human and a cat. In what way is the human skeleton similar to the cat skeleton? In what way is it different? Copy and complete this table. Look back at page 11 for help with the names of the human bones.

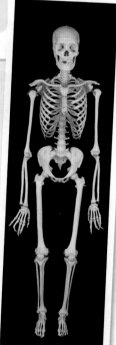

Which bones look similar?	Which bones look different?
Both skeletons have ribs.	*The cat skull is a different shape to the human skull.*

Did you know?

Some invertebrates such as ants, spiders, crabs, seahorses and lobsters have their skeleton on the outside. We call this type of skeleton an **exoskeleton**.

Challenge yourself!

A giraffe has the same number of bones in its neck as humans. How can this be possible? Write down your ideas.

Muscles help animals to move

Think like a scientist!

Did you know that animals need **muscles** to move? Bones cannot move on their own. We use muscles every time we move. Animals also use muscles to move.

Muscles work in pairs. For example, if you want to move your arm, two muscles work together. One muscle **contracts** (gets smaller) while the other muscle **relaxes** and becomes longer.
Look at the diagrams.

When you move your arm up, you contract the muscle on the upper arm – the **biceps**. You relax the muscle below – the **triceps**. When you stretch out your arm, you relax the muscle on your upper arm. You contract the muscle at the back of the arm.

Scientific words

muscles
contracts
relaxes
biceps
triceps

Arm bent

upper arm (biceps)

this muscle contracts
this muscle relaxes
back of arm (triceps)

Arm straight

this muscle relaxes
this muscle contracts

1

Look again at the diagram of the arm muscles contracting and relaxing.

a Use your own arm to copy what is happening in the diagram.

b Repeat what you have just done. This time, use your other hand to feel what is happening to your upper arm muscles.

c What can you feel when you stretch out your arm? And then, when you move your arm towards you?

2

Write down what happens when you move your arm up and down. Use these words to describe what the muscles are doing.

upper arm	back of arm
contract	relax
biceps	triceps

Moving muscles!

Think like a scientist!

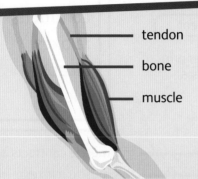

tendon

bone

muscle

Humans and animals have skeletons with muscles attached. Each muscle is attached to a different set of bones by **tendons**. You can feel your muscles change shape when you move. This diagram shows where the muscles are on the human body.

Where the muscles are on the human body

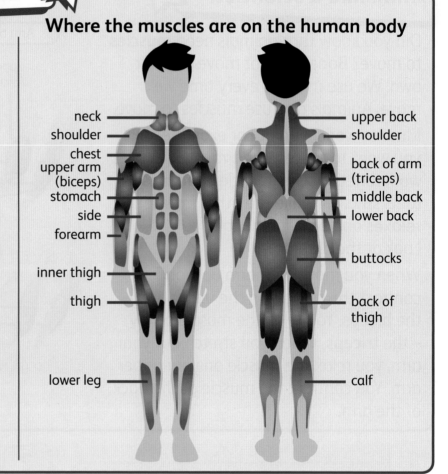

neck

shoulder

chest

upper arm (biceps)

stomach

side

forearm

inner thigh

thigh

lower leg

upper back

shoulder

back of arm (triceps)

middle back

lower back

buttocks

back of thigh

calf

1

Which bones are attached to the muscles in these places on the body? Use the diagram. **Hint:** If you need help with remembering the names of the bones, look back at the skeleton on page 11.

a thigh   **b** shoulder

c forearm   **d** lower back

e chest

Did you know?

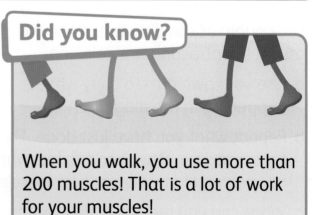

When you walk, you use more than 200 muscles! That is a lot of work for your muscles!

Scientific word

tendons

Making a model of your arm

1

You will need...
- cardboard • cardboard tubes
- scissors • tennis ball • elastic bands
- brass fasteners or paperclips

You are going to make a model of the muscles in the arm. Your model must show how the muscles contract (shorten) and act in pairs to help the bones in the arm move.

a Work with a partner. Look carefully at the diagrams of the arm muscles on pages 17 and 18. Also look at the diagram of the finished model, below.

b Your teacher will provide instructions on how you and your partner should make the model.

c When you have finished, show your model to the class. Decide who will explain how the model works. Discuss what to say using these words:

muscle	biceps	triceps
contract	relax	stretch
bones	arm	move

2

The heart is a special muscle. There are no other muscles like it in the body. The heart is the hardest-working muscle in your body. It never stops beating.

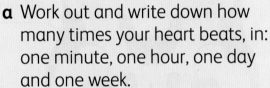

a Work out and write down how many times your heart beats, in: one minute, one hour, one day and one week.

b Some people need to have a 'pacemaker' fitted. Find out why. Research what a pacemaker is and what it does. Then explain your answer to a partner.

Did you know?

Did you know that your fingers do not have muscles in them? So how do you move your fingers? You use tendons, which are attached to muscles in your arm.

Joints

Think like a scientist!

In the body, a joint is where two or more bones meet. If the bones were stuck together, the muscles would not be able to make the bones move.

Muscles are linked to bones by strong tendons. When a muscle contracts, or gets shorter, it pulls on the bone. The bone can move if it is part of a joint. Elbow joints allow you to bend your arms at the elbow. Feel your elbow joint.

Your body has different kinds of joints. Look at the two types of joints shown here.

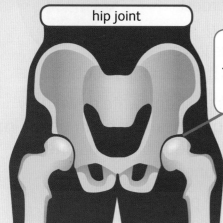

hip joint

A **ball-and-socket joint** allows the body to move bones in different directions.

A **hinge joint** moves just like the hinge on a door – backwards and forwards.

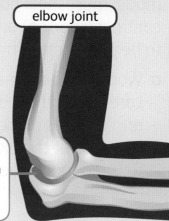

elbow joint

1

Think about the joints in your body.

a Where in your body do you have hinge joints?

b Where in your body to you have ball-and-socket joints?

Scientific words

ball-and-socket joint

hinge joint

record

Challenge yourself!

Here are some activities that involve using your joints. Do each activity and think carefully about which joints you are using. How will you **record** your answers? You could make a chart, or draw skeletons moving and label the joints. Or, take photographs and label the joints.

a running   **b** sitting

c writing   **d** bending your knees

e pretending to throw a ball

The role of medicines when the body is ill

Think like a scientist!

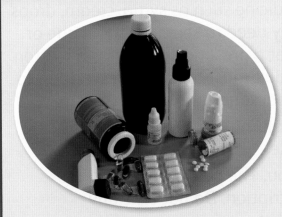

Medicines are sometimes called **drugs**. Medicines are substances that come in different forms, for example, syrup, cream, drops and tablets.

The medicines we take or use affect the body. For example, if you have a headache or fever (high temperature), an adult might give you medicine to help with the **symptoms**. Symptoms are signs that something is not right with your body when you are ill. Medicine may take away the headache or bring down the temperature.

Be careful

Only take medicine from an adult. Never take medicines yourself, without checking with an adult first.

Think about the medicines you have taken in the past.

Talk partners

Talk to a partner about what you both know about medicines. Discuss these questions:

a Why do we use medicines?

b Where do medicines come from?

c Have you ever taken medicines such as cough medicine? Which medicines and why?

d Is it safe to take medicines that belong to someone else? Why?

e Why do many people keep medicines in cupboards where children cannot reach them?

Scientific words

medicines

drugs

symptoms

Medicine safety

Think like a scientist!

When you are ill, you may need to take medicine such as syrup, cream, drops or tablets to help you to get better. You may need to see a doctor. If she or he prescribes a certain medicine, you will get a **prescription**. This is a written note with the details of the medicine. An adult must take the prescription to a **pharmacy** – a shop where a pharmacist packages and sells medicine.

If you simply have a cough or a cold, an adult may buy certain medicines from a supermarket, to help you to get better.

If you feel ill, always ask an adult to help you. The person may give you medicine or take you to a doctor for a prescription. Do not take any medicines without checking with an adult first.

1

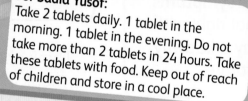

For Sadia Yusof:
Take 2 tablets daily. 1 tablet in the morning. 1 tablet in the evening. Do not take more than 2 tablets in 24 hours. Take these tablets with food. Keep out of reach of children and store in a cool place.

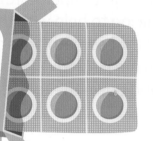

Scientific words

prescription

pharmacy

Look at the information on the box of medicine that the doctor gave Sadia. Write down the answers to these questions:

a What time of day should Sadia take her medicine?

b Should she take her medicine on an empty stomach (before eating)? How do you know?

c Where should Sadia keep the tablets? Why?

d How many tablets may Sadia take in 24 hours?

2

a Design a leaflet to explain:
- why medicines are important
- how to store medicines safely
- what information a medicine label has on it.

b Share your leaflet with a partner. Ask what is good about your leaflet and what you could improve.

What have you learnt about humans and animals?

1

Do you remember the body outline that you drew in the activity on page 10? Refer back to the outline to see what you did.

a Was everything on your outline correct? Add all the new things that you have learnt about the body. Go back to different pages in this unit to help you to think about what you want to add. Have you:

- drawn joints on the outline?
- drawn muscles? You might want to feel your own muscles in your body and draw what you feel.

b Look at the scientific words below and make sure that they are all on your outline.

muscles	hinge joint	ball-and-socket joint
thigh bone	biceps	triceps

stirrup (the smallest bone in your body)

What can you remember?

You have been learning about humans and animals. Can you:

- ✔ describe two things that the skeleton does?
- ✔ explain what the skull protects?
- ✔ explain what happens to your bones as you grow?
- ✔ point to your ribs, hips and wrist bones?
- ✔ explain how muscles make bones move?
- ✔ explain what medicines are and why they are important?
- ✔ describe how medicines should be stored safely at home?

Unit 2 Living things in their environment

What do you remember about different environments?

Think back to what you learnt about different environments. Read the following sentences. They will help to remind you that there are many different environments in the world:

- An environment is where humans, other animals, and plants live.
- There are different kinds of environments. Examples are mountains, deserts, forests, rivers and oceans.

1

This environment is a desert in India.

Scientific words
differences
similarities

This environment is a Malaysian rainforest.

Look carefully at the environment in each photograph.

a How many **differences** can you see in the two environments?

b How many **similarities** can you see? Copy and complete this table.

Similarities (things that are the same)	Differences (things that are different)

2

The Arctic region is around the North Pole.

a What is the environment like in the Arctic region?

b Draw a picture of yourself in the Arctic. What would you wear? Why?

c Pretend that you are looking through a pair of binoculars. Which of these animals would you see in the Arctic?

camel   polar bear   cobra

seal   scorpion   Arctic fox

Caring for our environment

What do you know about pollution? Think about this question when you do the activities on this page.

Talk partners

Look at the photograph.

a Talk to your partner about what the photograph shows.

b Listen to ideas from another pair.

c Were any of their ideas the same as yours? Explain your answer.

1

Read the conversation between Nor and Aisha.

a Do you agree with Nor or Aisha? Why?

b What do you think will happen to the animals and plants? Why?

c Why might the wastewater cause a problem?

d Draw some speech bubbles and write your ideas inside them.

I don't think the wastewater will hurt the environment.

I think the wastewater might hurt the environment, especially the animals and plants.

2

Imagine that you are walking with a friend. Your friend drops litter on the ground. What do you say to your friend? What if your friend answers you by saying: *I don't care?* Explain why litter is bad for the environment.

Habitats

Think like a scientist!

You are going to learn about **habitats**.

- The environment in which an animal or human lives is called its habitat.
- A habitat is a home – a place to live.
- Habitats have the things that animals (including humans) need to live:

  air (for some animals)   water

  food   **shelter**

  protection from **predators**
  (animals that eat other animals)

  a place to raise their young (babies).

Some habitats are big, for example, oceans and seas.

Some habitats are small, for example, a pond, a tree, or even under a rock.

Scientific words

habitats
shelter
predators

Challenge yourself!

With a partner, think of and name six habitats, small or big. Write them down. If you can think of more, well done!

1

Look at this picture of a frog in its habitat – a pond.

Why is a pond a good place for the frog to live? Write down your answer using the scientific words in the box.

Animals and their habitats

Think like a scientist!

Different animals live in different habitats.

Rabbits live in habitats that provide the things they need to live. A rabbit's habitat has grass to eat. There is also soil where they can burrow (dig) underground to create a safe place to live.

Rabbits are suited to living in their habitat. They have big ears to listen for predators. They also have an eye on each side of the head, so that they can see all around them.

Rabbits have strong muscles in their legs, so they can hop very fast and escape predators.

They have very sharp claws for digging burrows or warrens.

Rabbits live in groups in underground burrow systems called rabbit burrows or warrens.

Rabbits dig burrows and warrens underground for safety against predators.

There is grass for the rabbits to eat.

Burrows and warrens are sheltered, to raise young rabbits.

1

Earthworms live deep underground. Do some research on earthworms.

a Find out about the earthworm's: (habitat) (food) (predators) (young)

b How are earthworms suited to their habitat?

c Use your research to make an earthworm fact file.

Incredible habitats

Think like a scientist!

Many living things build incredible (unbelievable) homes!

Cathedral **termites** build their habitats in the shape of towers. The towers can be up to four metres tall and are made from mud, chewed wood, and termite **saliva**.

The towers are safe because the wind cannot blow them down. Predators such as birds find it hard to get inside. The towers are cool and moist because there are tubes inside. The tubes work like an air conditioner. The cool air from the bottom moves up to cool the warmer air at the top.

termite's habitat

1

You will need...

• tweezers • dough, mud or clay • stopwatch (or clock, timer or watch) • piece of card • camera

Scientific words

termites

saliva

prey

A predator is an animal that eats other animals. Animals that predators eat are called **prey**.

Incredibly, Cathedral termites build their habitats using their mouths. You are going to copy them and build a termite mound using only a pair of tweezers as a pretend mouth. How high can you build a tower in ten minutes?

a Use the tweezers to make the mound from dough, clay or mud on the piece of card.

b When you have finished, sketch or take a photograph the habitat.

c Write down three sentences to describe what it was like to make the habitat.

d Now that you have pretended to be a termite and have built a termite mound, what do you think of termites?

Habitats around your school

Think like a scientist!

There are many kinds of habitats. Some are big. Some are small. Some are simply incredible!

Rules for looking at habitats:

- Always treat living things with care.
- Do not damage any habitat.
- Always return animals to their habitat.
- Do not touch any plants or animals that might be poisonous.
- Always wash your hands when you have finished looking at a habitat.

Talk partners

Work with a partner. Walk around your school grounds. Make a list of the different habitats you see. How many did you find? Describe them.

Scientific words

annotate

invertebrates

record

1

You will need...

- clipboard • paper • pencil • hand lens

Go to your favourite habitat. Use a hand lens to observe the habitat carefully. What is it like?

a Is it in the shade or in the light? Is it damp or dry?

b What kind of animals and plants live there? Where is the food for the animals?

c What evidence of animals can you see?

d Sketch your habitat. Then **annotate** (label) your sketch with information.

2

Look for **invertebrates** (animals without backbones) such as woodlice, beetles, snails, slugs or worms in your habitat.

a Collect some invertebrates in a tray or plastic container.

b Observe them using a hand lens. **Record** what you can see.

c Sketch one of the invertebrates.

Another habitat in your school grounds

1

Choose a different habitat in your school grounds.

a Sketch or take a photograph of the habitat.

b Write down eight questions about your chosen habitat. The questions should help you to find out as much as you can. Start with these question stems:

- *What does …?*
- *Which …?*
- *What if …?*
- *Why …?*
- *Where …?*
- *How does …?*

c Use your sketch or photograph to write answers to your questions.
When you ask your questions, think about:

> animals   plants   food   shelter   predators
>
> temperature   light   shade   water

2

Make a diorama of your habitat in Activity 1. A diorama is a 3D scene. Look at the picture and talk to a partner about how it was made and what it shows.

a Make a list of what you will need. Then make the diorama.

b Show the diorama to someone else in your class. Share what you have found out about your habitat. Ask a partner to answer your eight questions from Activity 1.

Which habitat do invertebrates prefer?

 Think like a scientist!

Invertebrates are animals that do not have a skeleton inside them. [woodlouse] You may have seen invertebrates around your school and home. Examples are beetles, worms, woodlice, bees, wasps and flies.

1

Amal and Banke wanted to find out which habitat woodlice prefer. They did a survey to collect data about the number of woodlice in each habitat. They recorded what they saw by making notes about the environment of each habitat.

Here are their results:

Habitat	Environment			
	Dark and dry	Dark and damp	Light and dry	Light and damp
under a plant	1			
on a wall				
in a crack in the wall	6			
under stones		32		
under some wood		16		
under a pile of leaves		12		

Now answer these questions:

a What is the pattern in the results? **Hint:** Which environment do woodlice prefer?

b What environments are unsuitable for woodlice? Why?

Sorting animals and plants

Think like a scientist!

Do you know what **identify** means? To identify means to find out the name of something. **Identification** is something that we can recognise and that tells us, or identifies, who someone is or what something is.

Scientists sort animals and plants into groups and identify (name) them. Scientists do this by looking at the **similarities** and **differences** between animals and between groups.

Scientists identify and sort things into groups so that everyone can agree on the names and groups of animals and plants. This makes identifying animals and plants easier!

Challenge yourself!

Collect some leaves. How many ways can you sort the leaves? Think of a way to show your results and share your ideas with the class.

Scientific words
identify
identification
similarities
differences

1

You will need...
• some plastic animals or pictures of different animals

How many different ways can your sort your animals into groups? For example:

animals with four legs

animals with two legs

a Write down the different ways you sorted your animals. Then put the animals back together and sort them again.

b Try to find more than ten ways to sort the animals. Write them down.

Identification keys

Think like a scientist!

Scientists often need to find out the names of different plants and animals. To do this, they use an **identification key**. This special key helps them to sort and identify things quickly and easily.

1

Look at the Indian sweets. They look delicious, but if you do not know their names, how can you ask the shopkeeper for the sweets you want?

Use the identification key below to **classify** (sort) the sweets and find their names. Write down the name for each sweet.

Is it round?

YES

NO
burfi (also called barfi)

Does it look like a ball?

YES
gulab jamun

NO

Does it look like a ring?

NO
ras malai

YES
jalebi

Well done! You have classified these sweets and named each one. You have used an identification key.

Identifying living things

Think like a scientist!

There are millions of different kinds of living things on Earth. To identify them, scientists need to classify them. They sort them into groups and give them names. But, imagine sorting millions of things with no help!

Scientists have a way to make the job easier. They ask questions and look at the similarities and differences between things. This helps scientists to answer their questions and classify and identify the living things.

1

Use the identification key to match an animal to each letter below:

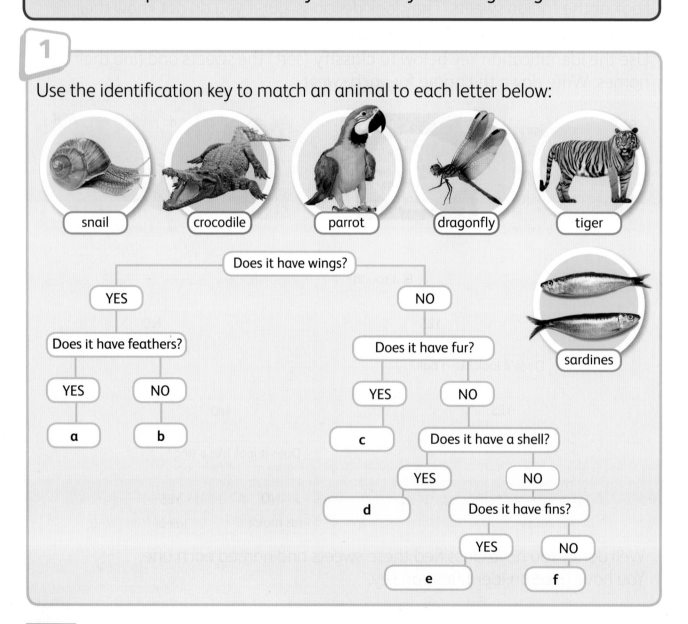

Using identification keys

Think like a scientist!

Scientists use identification keys to classify and identify plants or parts of plants. When scientists want to classify and name plants, they ask questions and look at the similarities and differences between things. This helps them to answer the questions and classify and identify the plants or plant parts.

1

Observe the leaves in the four photographs carefully.

a What similarities and differences can you see among the leaves?

b Compare the similarities and differences among the leaves to help you to name them using the identification key below.

c Ask a partner to check your answers.

i
ii
iii
iv

Challenge yourself!

Find some leaves in your school grounds. Research their names. Then create a key. Ask a partner to try out your key to identify the names of the leaves.

Is the leaf round?

YES → lily pad

NO → Does it have thin needle-shaped leaves?

YES → pine needles

NO → Is it dark on top and light underneath?

YES → olive leaf

NO → banana leaf

More about identification keys

1

Look at the identification key below. Someone has started to classify and identify the animals, but has forgotten to finish it.

a With your partner, work out how you will complete the identification key.

b Copy and complete the key. What will go in the empty boxes?

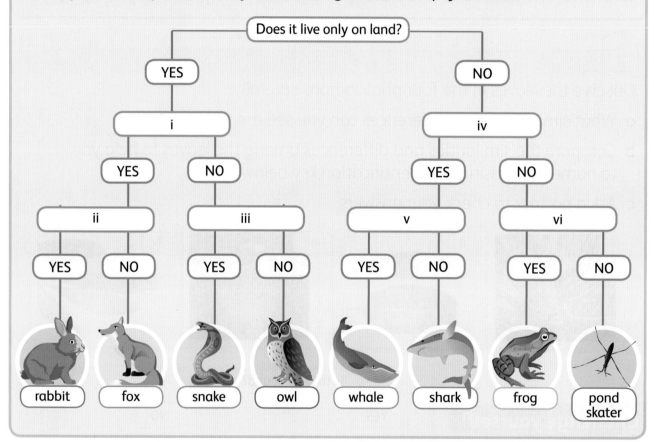

2

Choose some animals of your own. Make an identification key for your partner to use. Then give it to other pairs in your class to use.

Talk partners

Ask your partner to check the identification key to see if it works. Well done if it does! If it does not work, talk to your partner to work out why.

 Waste

Scientific word
billion

Think like a scientist!

Did you know that there are more than seven **billion** people on Earth now? And just think, each of those seven billion people creates waste. That is a lot of waste! Waste is anything that we throw away because we cannot use it or do not want it.

Some people, all over the world, try to reduce waste. These people know that too much waste causes pollution (dirties the environment). Pollution can be harmful to living things.

Talk partners

Think about all the waste we create. Talk to a partner. What do you think you could do about waste? Write down your ideas.

1

A group of children from a school in Malaysia created a 'Green team'. They decided to do something to prevent so much waste. The Green team decided that they need to:

- reduce waste
- reuse waste
- recycle waste.

What do the words mean?
Copy and complete the table .

Reduce, Reuse and Recycle

Word	My definition	Checked definition after using a dictionary or the internet	How good was my definition? 😠 Very good 🙂 Okay 🙁 Not very good
reduce			
reuse			
recycle			

Reduce, reuse, recycle

Think like a scientist!

Read the ideas of the Green team in Malaysia, to reduce, reuse and recycle waste:

1 Reduce
- Throw away less. Do not waste.
- Ask parents not to buy disposable cups or paper plates.
- Do not ask grown-ups to buy things that you do not really need.

2 Reuse
- Ask grown-ups to use plastic bags again and again.
- Reuse envelopes and write on both sides of paper.
- Use cardboard packaging such as egg boxes for other things like making models.

3 Recycle – turn waste into new things
- Ask grown-ups to put glass into a recycle bin, so new glass can be made.
- Ask grown-ups to take paper to a recycle bin. It can then be made into recycled (new) paper and card.
- Ask grown-ups to give their old spectacles to charities. Some charities recycle the glasses for people who cannot afford their own glasses.
- Give away or donate unwanted toys and clothes. There are people who will be able to use them.

1

Design and make your own Green team badge. Think about:
- What key words will you put on it?
- What colour will it be?
- What kind of picture could you put on it?

Talk partners

Would it be useful to have a Green team in your school? Talk to a partner and write down four reasons for your answer. Read how the Green team from Malaysia planned to reduce, reuse and recycle. What could you do? Write down your ideas.

Paper waste

Did you know?

Did you know that nearly one-quarter of the waste in a school is paper?

Sometimes schools throw away paper that has hardly been used … what a waste!

1

Read this email from the principal of the Malaysian school:

New Message	— x
From: principal@school.com	
To: green.team@school.com	

Subject: Reducing waste paper at school

Dear Green team,

I am concerned that we waste a lot of paper in our school. I would really like to reduce the amount that we throw away.

I would like to know:
- How much paper do classes in this school waste each day?
- How could we reduce the waste paper?

Please send your ideas to me as a short report. I look forward to reading your ideas for helping our school to reduce waste paper.

Best wishes
Mrs A School Principal

Send

Talk to a partner. How can you classify (sort) the waste paper in your class?

a Sort the waste paper into the three groups below. Think about how to measure the amount of waste paper in each group.

| Paper that has not been used at all | Paper that has only been used on one side | Paper that has been used on both sides |

b What are your **conclusions** after sorting the paper? How can your class reduce waste paper?

Waste paper chart

Think like a scientist!

The paper that you use at your school is made from trees:

- Tree fellers cut down the trees.
- Truck drivers use petrol to transport the trees to a paper mill.
- Mill workers use electricity to make the paper.
- Truck drivers use more petrol to transport the paper to your school.

paper mill

We use a lot of the resources on Earth to make paper – trees, petrol and electricity. If you and everyone else at your school use less paper, then you will all use less of the Earth's resources.

1

Use your results from the paper sort on page 39 to copy and complete the **bar chart**.

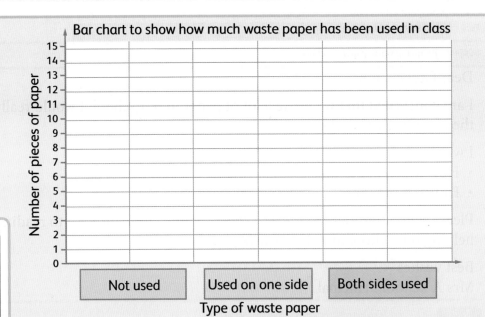

Bar chart to show how much waste paper has been used in class

Number of pieces of paper

| Not used | Used on one side | Both sides used |

Type of waste paper

Scientific word

bar chart

2

Talk to a partner about how paper is wasted. Also discuss what everyone in your class can do to reduce the waste.

Make a poster to persuade other learners to reduce waste paper in the classroom.

Challenge yourself!

Write a reply, in the form of a short report, to the email that the principal sent on page 39. Describe your ideas and what you have done to reduce waste paper in your class.

What else do we waste at school?

Think like a scientist!

Paper is not the only thing that we throw away at school. Schools also throw away metal, wood, plastic, card and other materials. Some of these materials cannot be used again, but some can. We can reuse some materials.

1

Your teacher will give you a bag of waste, collected at school.

a Sort the waste in different ways. Write labels to show how you have sorted the waste. If you have a camera, photograph each group of waste.

b Weigh the waste in each group. Record your results in a table like this:

The amount of waste at our school in one day	
Type of waste	**Weight of waste in one day (use g or kg)**

2

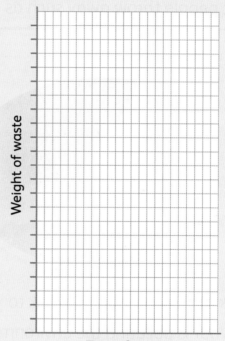

Amount of waste at our school in one day

Weight of waste

Type of waste

Present the information from Activity 1 in a bar chart to show the weight of waste in each group at your school.

a Copy and complete the chart.

b Look at the results in your chart and write your conclusions underneath it.

 **Pollution**

Scientific words
pollution
contaminated
oil tanker

 Think like a scientist!

Sometimes, people damage the environment by throwing waste into it. You might have seen news about **pollution** on the internet, TV or in newspapers. Pollution happens when the environment is **contaminated** (dirtied) by waste.

The waste might be chemicals from factories and farms. It might be from an **oil tanker** spilling oil into the sea. The waste might be car fumes or rubbish such as broken shopping trolleys. It might be old furniture and other things that people throw away such as plastic bags and bottles.

1

Look at the photographs. Talk to your partner about them.

a What is polluting the environment in each picture? Write down your answers.

b Why is the pollution in each picture bad for the environment?

c How do you think the pollution could be stopped?

d Share your ideas with another pair of learners in your class. Are their ideas the same as yours, or different?

Effects of pollution

1

Think about the area where you live. Have you seen any pollution?

a Talk to a partner about the kind of pollution you have seen.

b Draw a picture of the pollution you have seen. If you have a camera, take a photograph.

c What is polluting the environment in your picture? Write down how you think those things got there.

d Write down your ideas about how the pollution could affect humans and other animals.

e Why will it be better for everyone if we stop polluting this area?

Think like a scientist!

Sometimes careless people cause damage to the environment. Perhaps you have heard of pollution caused by an **oil spill**?

An oil spill happens when people make mistakes or are careless on a ship that transports oil (an oil tanker).

Oil leaks from the tanker into the ocean, sometimes very near the shore.

The black oil floats on top of water and washes up onto beaches. Many animals are harmed and even die, because:

- Animals' skin, feathers and fur are covered in oil so they cannot swim or fly easily.
- Oil gets into animals' stomachs and **poisons** them.
- Oil gets into animals' eyes and blinds them.

Scientific words

oil spill

poisons

a sea otter trying to swim in thick oil on the water

Oil spills

Think like a scientist!

Oil can spill into seas or rivers by accident. Oil spills can affect the environment. Therefore, people must clean up the oil spills quickly.

Look at the top photograph. Booms (long tubes that are filled with air) keep oil spills in one place. Then ships use machines to suck the oil from the surface (top) of the water.

Look at the bottom photograph. Sometimes people in small planes spray special chemicals on oil spills. The chemicals break down the oil.

boom

oil spill

chemical spray

oil spill

1

Investigate the best way to clean an oil spill. Work with a partner.

You will need...
- cup of cooking oil
- water
- straw or dry grass
- washing-up liquid
- fabric
- bowl
- sand
- sawdust
- cotton wool
- newspaper

a Make your own oil spill. Pour some cooking oil into a bowl of water.

b How will you clean up the oil spill? Use the items in the list, or other items you think you need.

Think about these questions:
- *What will you do?*
- *Must you start over again after each test?*
- *How will you know how much oil you have cleaned up after each test? What will you measure?*
- *How will you record your results?*

c At the end, write a report to explain what you did. Draw and label a diagram of how well each test worked. Write your conclusions under the diagram. Describe the best way to clean up an oil spill.

Cleaning oil off sea otter fur

1

You will need...

- half a cup of cooking oil
- half a cup of water
- beaker or container
- washing-up liquid
- toothbrush
- spoon
- fake fur
- tray

Oil spills affect animals in the environment such as sea otters. On page 44 you investigated the best way to clean up an oil spill. This time, investigate the best way to clean oil from fake fur.

a Soak some fake fur in oily water. Draw a plan of the best way to remove the oil.

b Very carefully, clean the oil off the fur. Imagine that the fur is on a real sea otter, so you must not damage it. If you damage its fur, the sea otter will not be able to survive.

c Is it a difficult job? Why do you think it would be difficult to clean oil off the fur of a sea otter or other animal? Write down four reasons.

Challenge yourself!

Find out about how oil pollution (or another form of pollution) has affected a river in your country in the past.

a What happened?

b How did it affect wildlife?

c How did it affect humans?

2

Oil is not the only thing that can harm animals. Plastic can be very dangerous for animals.

a Find out how plastic pollution, especially plastic bags, can harm animals.

b Design a poster to encourage people to use fewer plastic bags and dispose (get rid) of them properly.

What have you learnt about living things in their environment?

1

rainforest   ocean

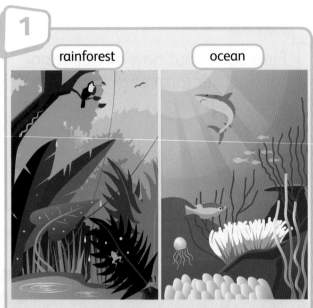

Look at the pictures of two different environments.

Write down three similarities and three differences between them.

2

a Look at the photograph of the spider monkey. How do you think it is suited to living in its habitat?

b Write down four ways in which it is suited to its environment.

What can you remember?

You have been learning about living things in their environment. Can you:

✔ name four different habitats?

✔ say which animals live in a habitat in your school?

✔ say why the animals live there?

✔ use an identification key to identify animals and leaves?

✔ tell someone what 'reduce', 'reuse' and 'recycle' means?

✔ tell someone about how you help to reduce waste?

✔ tell someone what pollution is?

✔ tell someone how oil pollution is harmful to animals?

1 Humans and some animals have bony skeletons inside their bodies.

   a Use these words to label the human skeleton: kneecap, skull, backbone, thigh bone, wrist, ribcage, pelvis, ankle. Write the letters and the labels.

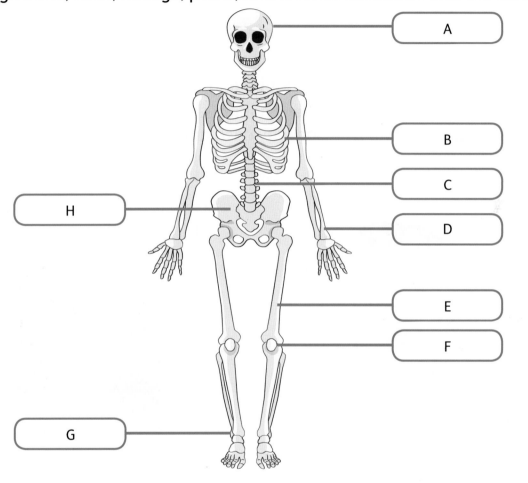

A

B

C

H

D

E

F

G

(8)

   b Which part protects the heart and lungs?   (1)
   c True or False? Bones do not grow as humans grow.   (1)

2 Which diagram shows the upper arm (bicep) muscle contracting – **a** or **b**? (1)

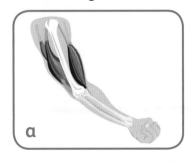

a

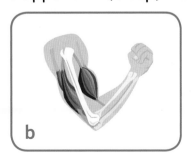

b

3 Name two bones that have muscles attached to them.   (2)

4 Are these statements true or false?
   Write a to e and True or False next to each letter.

   a All drugs are medicines.

   b Anyone can prescribe medicines.

   c Medicines should be kept in a safe place.

   d Medicines help people to get better.

   e It is safe to take medicines that belong to someone else.   (5)

5 Different animals live in different habitats. Match each animal to the
   correct habitat. Write a reason why each animal is suited to its habitat.

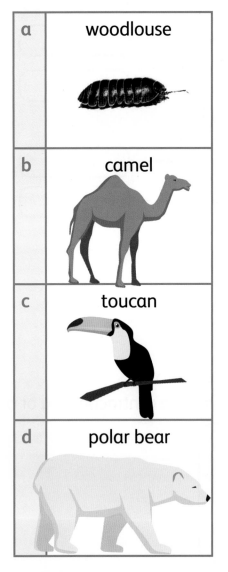

a	woodlouse	i	
b	camel	ii	
c	toucan	iii	
d	polar bear	iv	

          (4)

6 Sarah and Hiba carried out an investigation to find out which habitat woodlice like best. The bar chart shows their results. Use the results in the chart to answer these questions.

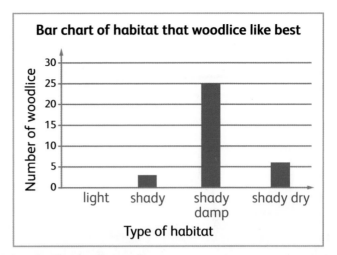

Bar chart of habitat that woodlice like best

a Which habitat had zero woodlice in it?

b How many woodlice were in the shady damp habitat?

c Why were there no woodlice in the light habitat?

d Look at the chart. What is your conclusion about where woodlice like to live? Complete this sentence: My conclusion is _____ because _____ .   (4)

7 Use the key below to identify the four animals. Write the correct animal for each letter.

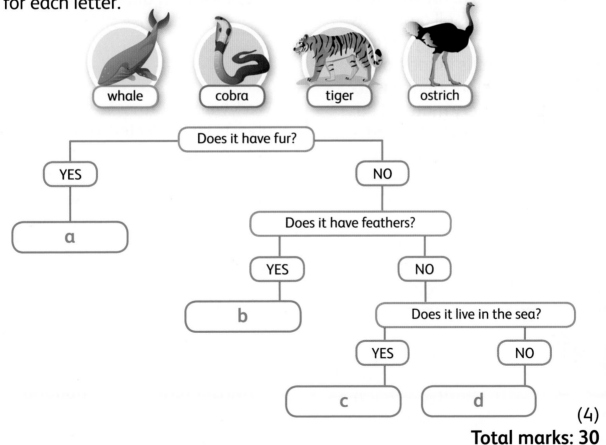

Total marks: 30

What do you know about materials?

Think like a scientist!

Everything is made of some kind of **material**. There are different kinds of materials all around us. Look around you. Can you find something that is made from wood, metal, fabric and plastic? Name them. Every material has **properties**, for example, hard, soft, shiny, smooth, rough or prickly.

Scientific words

material properties soft dull shiny waterproof transparent opaque flexible rigid

Why do runners carry their water in plastic bottles rather than glass bottles?

Talk partners

With a partner, collect five objects from around the classroom. The objects must be made from different materials. Sort them according to what they are made from. You may find that some objects are made from the same material. Make a list of the different ways you have sorted your objects. Share your list with another pair.

1

Work with a partner to sort the five objects you collected into groups according to their properties. Decide on the sorting groups first. Below are some ideas. Use the scientific dictionary on pages 140 to 144 if you are unsure about the meaning of a word.

soft	dull
shiny	waterproof
transparent	opaque
flexible	rigid

Silly materials

1

You know a lot about materials. Now use what you know to have some fun! What is the silliest material that you could use to make an object? One has been done for you.

chocolate coffee pot

a Why is a coffee pot made from chocolate silly?

b What would be the silliest things that you could make from:

chocolate   concrete   paper   glass

Copy and complete this table.

Material	What could you make that would be silly? Why?
chocolate	*coffee pot, it would melt*
concrete	
paper	
glass	

Scientific words

magnetic

non-magnetic

2

Remember that some materials are **magnetic** and some are not (**non-magnetic**). This means that a magnet can pick up some materials and not others.

a Here are some objects made from different materials:

steel wire paperclips   stainless steel spoon   aluminium drinks can

aluminium saucepan   gold ring   nickel-covered scissors   plastic bag

Predict if each one is magnetic or non-magnetic. Why?

b Find out if your prediction for each material is correct.

States of matter

Think like a scientist!

You are now going to learn about **states of matter. Matter** is everything we are made of and everything that is around us. Matter is all the different materials we see and use. This includes what you drink, the chair you are sitting on and the air you are breathing right now. The different states of matter are in the forms of **solid**, **liquid** or **gas**.

1

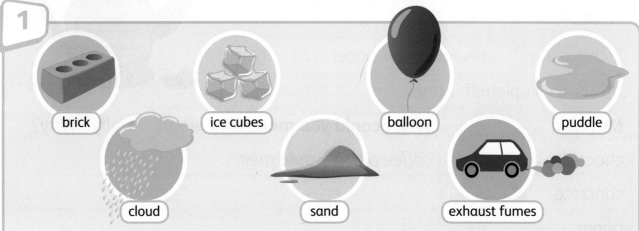

brick   ice cubes   balloon   puddle

cloud   sand   exhaust fumes

Everything in these pictures is made of matter. Matter can be in the form of a solid, a liquid or a gas.

a Talk about each picture. Is it a solid, a liquid or a gas?

b Copy and complete the table. Write each object in the correct column. If you are unsure, use the 'Not sure' column.

Solid	Liquid	Gas	Not sure

Talk partners

Talk to a partner about the things that you put in each column. Did you put some things in the 'Not sure' column? Write down your reasons.

Scientific words

states of matter
matter
solid
liquid
gas

What is a solid?

Think like a scientist!

In Activity 1 on page 52, you sorted solids, liquids and gases. Think about the things you put in the 'Solid' column.

A solid is something that keeps its shape, for example, a brick. It cannot be poured like a liquid.

Imagine that you put salt, sand or sugar into a container. It may look as if they are being poured. However, each grain (piece) of sand, salt and sugar is a solid, not a liquid. They are not really being poured. They are being piled up inside the container.

We can change the shape of a solid such as bread dough if we use a big enough force.

brick

liquid

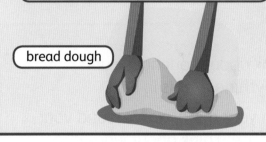
what salt looks like under a microscope

bread dough

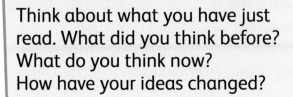

Talk partners

Think about what you have just read. What did you think before? What do you think now? How have your ideas changed?

1

Collect six solids from around your classroom. Make a display.

a Make a label for your display. Explain why each object in your display is a solid.

b Ask other learners to look at your display. Do they agree that each object is a solid? Do they think your explanations are good?

Everyday things that are solids

Think like a scientist!

Matter can be a solid. Remember: a solid keeps it shape (unless we change it using force) and cannot be poured.
Solids are all around us. Your hair is a solid. Your shoes are a solid.

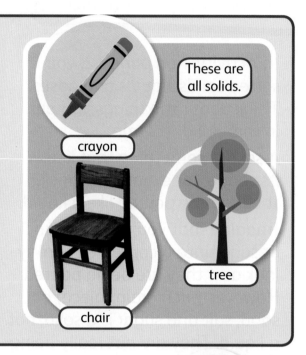

These are all solids.

crayon

chair

tree

1

Draw a picture of yourself. Label some things on you that are solids.

2

Think about your house and everything that is in it.

a In your mind, walk around your house. Think about what is in each room.

b Draw a house. Inside each room write the name of a solid, a liquid, and a gas. Explain why each thing is a solid, a liquid or a gas.

Are your finger nails solids?

3

During this unit you will make three fact cards. They should be about the states of matter. Make one about solids. Make one about liquids, and one about gases.

Make the first card about SOLIDS. Describe what a solid is. Give examples of three objects that are made from solid materials.

What is a liquid?

Think like a scientist!

You have learnt about why some things can be **classified** (grouped) as solids. Now you will learn about liquids.

We can tell if something is a liquid because:

- We can pour a liquid easily.
- A liquid is not easy to hold.
- Liquids change their shape. They take the shape of their containers. If you pour a liquid into a glass it will take the shape of the glass.

Scientific word
classified

1

You will need...
- bowl
- different-shaped containers
- water

Pour water into different-shaped containers.

a What do you notice about what the water does?

b Try to hold liquid in your hand. Hold your hand over a bowl. Pour water into your hand. What does the water do in your hand?

Challenge yourself!

Think about all the liquids you have at home. Also think about liquids near your home.

a Make a list of all the liquids.

b Use your list to make an interesting poster.

c Share your poster with your group. What do they think of your ideas? What is your most interesting liquid?

Runny liquids

Scientific word
viscosity

Think like a scientist!

Not all liquids are the same. They can be different colours. They can have different smells. Some liquids are runnier than others. We say they have a different **viscosity**.

1

water | cooking oil | treacle | shampoo

Your teacher will give you four small plastic bottles. Each bottle contains a different liquid. Look at the liquids in the bottles. Do not touch the bottles.

a With your partner, predict which liquid is the runniest. Write down your prediction.

b Now find out if your prediction is correct. Move the liquid around in the bottles. Do not remove the caps. Put the liquids in order from most runny to least runny.

c Is your prediction correct?

What liquids are in your body?

Runny liquids investigation

Think like a scientist!

Manufacturers make products such as tomato ketchup and shampoo. They need to make sure that their products are the right **consistency**. Products must not be too runny or too thick. If they are too runny, the products would pour out too quickly. If the products are too thick, they would be difficult to pour from the bottles.
How quickly or slowly a liquid flows is called its viscosity.

Scientific words

manufacturers

consistency

variables

factors

record

conclusions

1

You will need...

- metal or plastic tray
- water
- cooking oil
- treacle
- shampoo
- stopwatch
- spoon

Carry out an investigation using a fair test. Find out which liquid from Activity 1 on page 56 is the runniest. Senara and Keeya planned their fair test using a diagram like this:

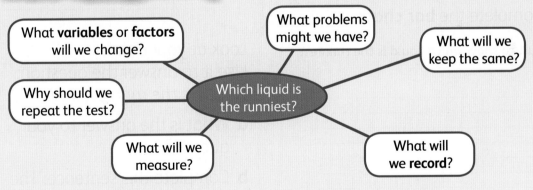

a Copy the diagram. Answer the questions to plan a fair test.

b Look at your plan. Check that you have planned:

- to predict what will happen, and any problems
- to take some measurements
- a table to record your results.

c Carry out your fair test and record your results.

d Repeat the test. Did you get the same results? What are your **conclusions**?

Investigation results

Think like a scientist!

Scientists always collect evidence of what happened during investigations. They do this in various ways. They take measurements. They record the measurements (results) in a table. Sometimes they use the results to draw a graph or a chart.

Scientific word
bar chart

Use this to remember which way the axes go:
x **to the right**   and   *y* **to the sky**

1

On page 57 you carried out a fair test. You found out which liquid was the runniest. Use your results to copy and complete the **bar chart**.

Bar chart to show which liquid is the runniest

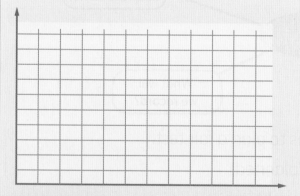

Remember:
- On the *x*-axis, put what you changed.
- On the *y*-axis, put what you measured (your result).

2

Look at your chart.
Use it to answer the question:
Which is the runniest liquid?

a What is the answer to your question?

b Complete this sentence: The runniest liquid is _____ because _____.

3

Make a LIQUIDS fact card. Look back at page 54 to remind yourself how to do this.

What is a gas?

Scientific word
oxygen

Think like a scientist!

Gases are everywhere. Most of the time we do not know that they are there.

- Gases are usually invisible. This means that we cannot see them.
- The air that you breathe is made up of different gases such as **oxygen**, which is colourless and odourless (does not have any smell).
- Gases move around and fill spaces. They can change their shape. Wave your hand. You are waving your hand though invisible gases!

1

Work with a partner. Blow into a paper bag.

You will need...
- paper bag

a Is there anything in the bag?

b How do you know? What is in the bag?

2

You will need...
- balloon (inflated – blown or pumped up)
- balloon (not inflated)

Work with your partner again.

a Compare two balloons. One balloon should be inflated. The other should not. Feel the balloons. How are they similar and different?

b Use the balloon that has been inflated. Can you squash the balloon? How can you turn it into different shapes?

c What is inside this balloon? How do you know?

3

You will need...
- bicycle pump (if possible)
- balloon (not inflated)

Use a bicycle pump to fill the balloon with air. Or, use your breath to blow up the balloon. Push out the air onto your arm. How do you know there was air in the pump (or in your breath)?

Be careful

Do not push the air out into your face!

Gases are everywhere

Think like a scientist!

On page 59 you found out that gases are everywhere. Air is made up of different gases. The gases are mainly oxygen, carbon dioxide and nitrogen. There was air in the balloon and the bicycle pump. We breathe in air all day, every day.

1

Is there anything in the empty drinks can?

You will need...
- empty drinks can
- bowl of water
- empty plastic bottle

a Talk to a partner. What do you think is in the empty drinks can?

b Predict what will happen when you push the drinks can into the bowl of water? Try it and see if you are right.

c What comes out of the can? Why?

d Write down your ideas.

e Try this activity again with an empty plastic bottle. Predict what will happen first. Were you right?

Challenge yourself!

Choose two activities from this page and page 59. Demonstrate them to your partner to prove:
- Gases are everywhere.
- Gases are usually invisible.
- Gases can take up any space.

2

You will need...
- bubble mixture
- bubble blowers

Do this activity outside. With your partner, blow some bubbles.

a Explain how to make a bubble. What are you blowing into the bubble? Where is it coming from?

b How can you make bigger and smaller bubbles?

c Where does the air (gas) go when the bubble bursts?

Making a gas

1

You will need...
- transparent bottle
- bicarbonate of soda
- vinegar
- teaspoon
- plastic glove

When some materials mix they make a gas. When you mix bicarbonate of soda with vinegar, a change takes place. Try this activity:

a Add a little vinegar to the transparent bottle. Fill the finger of a plastic glove with a teaspoon of bicarbonate of soda.

b Carefully stretch the glove over the top of the bottle. Be careful not to spill any bicarbonate of soda into the bottle.

c Predict what you think will happen when you lift the finger of the glove and add the bicarbonate of soda to the vinegar. Draw a diagram of your prediction.

d Now try it.

e Draw a new diagram to show what happened.

f Compare your first diagram with the second diagram. Was your prediction correct? Write a sentence under each diagram. Explain what happened when you mixed the solid bicarbonate of soda with the liquid vinegar.

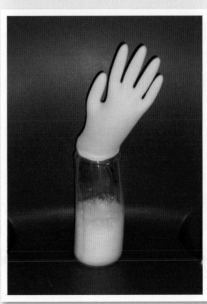

Practise naming the states of matter

1

You have learnt that there are three states of matter. These are solid, liquid and gas. Look at the things in **a** to **i**. In which state is each object – solid, liquid or gas? Write down your answers.

2

Make a 'States of matter' GASES fact card.
Look back at page 54 to remind yourself how to do this.

Use all the scientific words you have learnt in your fact card. Go back to pages 59 to 61 to remind yourself of the words.

How many words to do with states of matter can you remember?

 Boiling water

Think like a scientist!

When a substance changes from one state of matter (such as a solid) to another state of matter (such as a liquid), we call this a **change of state**.

- Imagine water in its liquid state. When we cool it to freezing point (0°C), it changes state to become a solid (ice). (Note: the C stands for Celsius.)

- Imagine water as a solid (ice). When we heat it (above 0°C), it melts. It changes state to a liquid.

- When we heat water to its boiling point (100°C), it changes state to become a gas. The gas between the spout of the kettle and the **steam** is called **water vapour** and is invisible.

- As the water vapour and steam cools, it changes state back into a liquid. We call this **condensing**.

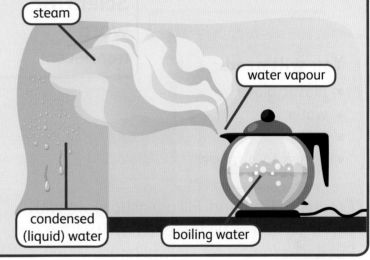

steam

water vapour

condensed (liquid) water

boiling water

1

Class 4 watched their teacher heat water in a kettle until it boiled. They observed the steam coming out of the kettle. The teacher held a cold metal tray over the steam. The steam changed back to water.

Draw pictures to show each stage of the process. Label your pictures. Use these words and any others that you think are important.

steam	boiling	kettle
gas	liquid	water vapour

Scientific words

change of state

steam

water vapour

condensing

Ice sculptures

Think like a scientist!

Ice is a solid. Ice is water that has been cooled to 0 °C or below. At this temperature, the water freezes and changes from a liquid to a solid.

Did you know?

There are ice sculpture competitions all over the world. People change the shape of huge blocks of ice to make amazing ice sculptures.

1

Scientific word
translucent

You will need...
- plastic glove
- water
- peg
- access to a freezer

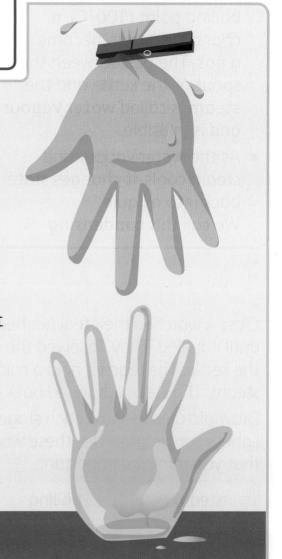

Create an ice hand. Fill a plastic glove with water. Fasten or tie the end firmly with a peg. Put it in a freezer for several hours. When frozen, carefully peel off the plastic glove. You will have an ice hand!

a Explore the ice hand. What can you find out about it? What is the ice like?

b Is the ice transparent, **translucent** or opaque?

c Can you see any bubbles in the ice hand? What do you think is inside the bubbles?

d Which parts of the hand will melt first? Why?

e Why do different parts of the hand take different times to melt?

Melting ice

Think like a scientist!

Ice is water that has frozen. It has changed from a liquid to a solid.

If we heat ice, it will change from a solid to a liquid. We call this melting. Ice melts when the temperature is above 0 °C. We use a thermometer to measure temperature.

Remember: Do not hold a thermometer where the liquid inside it is. If you do, you will measure the temperature of your hand!

1

Lia and Alec have different ideas about ice melting. Do you agree or disagree with their ideas? Explain why to your partner.

I don't think the temperature makes any difference.

Ice cubes melt faster when the temperature is higher.

a Plan an investigation with your partner. Find out who is correct – Lia or Alec? Think about:

- How will you keep your comparison fair?
- What will you change?
- What will you measure?
- How will you record your results?

b Predict what will happen and write down your ideas.

c Carry out your investigation and record the results. Is your prediction correct?

d Finally, draw and annotate (label) a diagram showing what you did.

Do all solids melt at the same time?

Be careful !

Scientists need to know how to work safely. Before they begin investigations, they think about safety.

When using a flame, work like a scientist. Follow these safety rules:

- Do not touch the flame.
- Tie back long hair.
- Keep clothes out of the way.
- Do not touch anything that is hot.

1

You will need...

- tea light
- small foil cake cases
- butter or margarine
- tea light holder
- pieces of chocolate
- tray of sand
- stopwatch
- wax
- goggles

Investigate which of these solids will melt fastest: chocolate wax butter

a Plan your investigation with a partner. Think about these questions:
- How will you make your test fair and safe?
- What will you measure?
- Why should you repeat the test?
- How will you record your results?

b Before you begin, predict which solid will melt fastest.

c Carry out your fair test. As you melt each solid, observe how it melts. Record your results. If you have a camera, take photographs of your test.

d Look at your results. Was your prediction correct?

e Repeat the test. Were your results the same?

f Use your observations to write four sentences to describe how each solid melted. You could use your photographs as a reminder. What are your conclusions? Use these words in your sentences:

| solid | liquid | melt | soften |
| harden | changed | similar | different |

Changing from liquid to solid

Think like a scientist!

When we heat some materials they melt (become liquid). To melt a material we must heat it. As the liquid cools, it becomes a solid again. We say that the liquid has **solidified**. This is called a **reversible change**. The solid melts. As it cools, it becomes a solid again.

Scientific words
solidified
reversible change

1

In this activity, you will observe butter in two states: solid and liquid.

You will need...
- tea light
- tea light holder
- butter
- stopwatch
- metal spoon
- tweezers
- greaseproof paper or small foil cases

Be careful

Follow the safety rules on page 66.

a Use a tea light to melt the butter. Refer to your notes and what you did in the activity on page 66. Observe the changes that take place.

b Pour the butter onto a sheet of greaseproof paper, or, pour it into foil cases. Use the back of a metal spoon to shape the butter. Leave the butter to cool. Observe that you have created your own butter shape! Use tweezers to peel the greaseproof paper or foil cases off the butter.

c When is the butter in these states of matter? solid → liquid → solid

2

Think back to the steps in Activity 1. Draw four pictures showing the states of matter of the butter. Under each picture write one or more of these words:

solid   liquid   reversible change   melted   solidified

Reversible and irreversible change

Think like a scientist!

Watch your teacher light a candle. The wick will burn and the candle wax will melt.
The liquid candle wax runs down the side of the candle and cools. It then changes from a liquid to a solid. The change in the wax is a reversible change.

flame

wick

liquid wax

solid wax

Some materials do not change back to the same state after heating. We call this an **irreversible change**. For example, imagine heating a raw egg to cook it. You cannot change the egg back into its raw state.

cooked egg

Scientific word

irreversible change

1

You will need...
• tray of sand
• candle

Be careful !

Follow the safety rules on page 66.

Observe what happens as a candle burns. Work with a partner.

a Place the candle firmly into the tray of sand. Your teacher will light the candle for you. Remember the safety rules!

b Observe the candle. Draw the candle after it has burned for few minutes. Write your observations around your drawing.

c Write what you can smell, hear and see. Do not lean too close to the burning candle!

d How does the candle wax change? Write sentences to explain what is happening. Remember to use these words:

solid	liquid	melt
solidify	reversible	change

Challenge yourself!

Make a list of things that cannot be changed back after heating and cooling.

What have you learnt about states of matter?

1

What have you learnt about states of matter? Think about it.

a Work with a partner. Tell each other three things you know about a solid, a liquid and a gas.

b Now draw three speech bubbles. Write down what you said to your partner. Your speech bubbles must describe solids, liquids, and gases.

I think
a solid
_____

I think
a liquid
_____

I think
a gas
_____

c Show your partner the speech bubbles. Does your partner agree with what you wrote? Ask your partner to suggest how to improve what you wrote.

What can you remember?

You have been learning about states of matter. Can you:

✔ say what the three states of matter are?
✔ tell someone what happens when a solid is heated?
✔ tell someone what happens when a liquid is cooled?
✔ describe what happens when a liquid is heated?
✔ describe what happens when water vapour is cooled?
✔ say if freezing is a reversible change or an irreversible change?

Practice test 2: Chemistry

1 Which of these materials is a solid, a liquid or a gas?

   a water vapour   b apple juice   c concrete   d water

   e brick   f air   g wood   h oxygen   (8)

2 Malaki left a bar of chocolate on a sunny windowsill.

   a Describe what happened to the chocolate.

   b How can Malaki change the chocolate back to a solid?   (3)

3 Match the correct word to the labels on the diagram.:

| water vapour | | condensation | | boiling water | | steam | (4)

4 Class 4 investigated: 'Which substance melts the fastest?'
Here are some sentences from their report.
Read the sentences. Which sentence is a:

  • conclusion?   • prediction?   • result?

   a We think the candle wax will melt the fastest.

   b The butter melted in six seconds.

   c The substance that melted fastest was butter.   (3)

5 Melting is the reverse of freezing.

   a What must you do to change an ice cube into water?

   b What must you do to change water into an ice cube?

   c Is freezing a reversible or irreversible change?   (3)

6 Look at the diagram of changes in state. Match the correct word to each label on the diagram.

   water vapour (gas)   solid ice   boil   water (liquid)   freeze

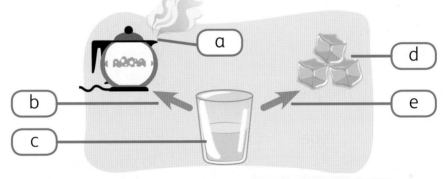

(5)

7 Class 4 investigated to find out which liquid was the runniest. Here are their results.

Liquid	Time to flow down tray in seconds
water	4
treacle	24
cooking oil	16
shampoo	19

   a Which liquid was the runniest?

   b Which liquid was the slowest?

   c What did they measure?

   d Write one thing that you think Class 4 kept fair when they did their test. (4)

Total marks: 30

Unit 4 Magnetism

What do you know about magnets?

1

Scientific word
bar magnet

You will need...
• sheet of paper

What do you already know about magnets?

Draw a large **bar magnet** on a sheet of paper. Add what you know about magnets.
Use these words:

attract	magnetic
metals	repel

Magnets can be ...

2

You are going to learn more about magnets. First, make a 'Magnet book' for all the information.

a Plan your book on a sheet of paper. Think about and answer these questions:

- What will your book look like?
- What shape will it be?
- What will you put on the front cover?
- Where will the contents page be?
- Do you need a glossary at the end, for scientific words?
- Will you have a 'Fascinating facts' page?

b Now make your Magnet book. Use it as you complete each activity. Write, draw and stick pictures and photographs in the book. Add anything extra that you find out about magnets.

Be careful !

In your Magnet book, write these safety rules about magnets:
- Do not drop or bang magnets – they might lose their magnetism.
- After using a horseshoe magnet, replace (put back) the metal keeper – a piece of metal that goes across the ends to keep the strength of a magnet.
- Do not use magnets near mobile phones, interactive whiteboards, computers or any other digital devices.

What is a magnet?

Think like a scientist!

As you work through this unit, you will learn that:
- A magnet is usually made from metal.
- Magnets are objects that produce an area of **magnetic force** called a **magnetic field**.
- Magnetic fields are invisible. We cannot see them.

Scientific words
magnetic force
magnetic field
mind map

1

You will need...
- different kinds of magnets
- collection of everyday objects
- timer

Work with a partner to explore the magnets. Discover as much as you can about what magnets do.

a You have ten minutes to explore the magnets. So, set the timer and start!

b What did you find out? Create a **mind map** showing what you discovered. If you need to check something, try it again with the magnets.

c What was the most interesting thing you found out?

d Show your mind map to another pair. Did they find out similar things? Did they discover anything that you did not?

e Write down what you found out, in your Magnet book.

Challenge yourself!

How many magnets can you find at home? What are they used for? Take photographs or draw pictures in your Magnet book.

What happens when you put two magnets together?

What do magnets attract?

Think like a scientist!

Think back to exploring magnets in Activity 1 on page 73. You probably learnt that magnets pull some things towards them. Scientists say that magnets **attract** materials. And, some materials are **attracted** to a magnet. Things that are attracted to magnets are made from **magnetic** materials.

1

Scientific words

attract
attracted
magnetic
Venn diagram
non-magnetic

You will need...

- some magnets
- objects made from different materials
- two hoops

Which materials are attracted to magnets?

a Overlap the two hoops. This creates a **Venn diagram** with two sorting areas: magnetic and **non-magnetic**. Sort the objects into the correct areas.

b Did any objects have magnetic and non-magnetic parts? Where will you place these in the diagram?

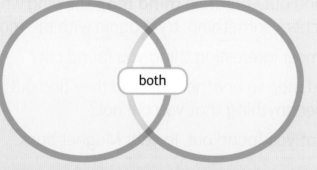

magnetic   both   non-magnetic

c Think about the materials from which the objects are made.
What materials are the magnetic objects made from?
What materials are the non-magnetic objects made from?

d Write a list of the materials that are magnetic.

e Write a list of the materials that are non-magnetic.

Do magnets attract all kinds of metals?

Think like a scientist!

Think back to Activity 1 on page 74. Did you notice that **metal** objects were attracted to the magnets? Magnets attract some metals. Scientists say that these metals are magnetic. But not all metals are attracted to magnets. You are going to investigate magnetic and non-magnetic metals.

1

You will need...

- objects made from different metals (for example, aluminium can, iron bolt, copper wire, a nickel coin, silver bracelet)
- magnet

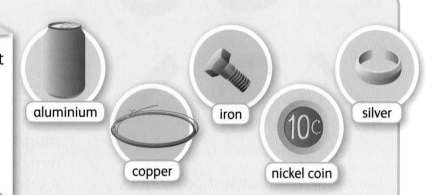

aluminium   copper   iron   10¢ nickel coin   silver

Collect objects made from different metals. Try to find objects made from these metals: **aluminium** **iron** **copper** **silver** **nickel**

a What type of metal is each object? Find out and label it.

b Plan your investigation with a partner. Which of your metals are magnetic? Which metals are not? What will you do?
How will you **record** your results?

c When you have finished, look at your results.
What is your **conclusion**? What kinds of metals are attracted to magnets?

Scientific words

metal
aluminium
iron
copper
silver
nickel
record
conclusion

2

In your Magnet book, write down five things about magnets. Explain these words in your glossary:

magnet   attract   magnetic

All kinds of magnets

1

Look at the magnets and the names below. Copy and complete the table. Match each magnet name with the correct letter.

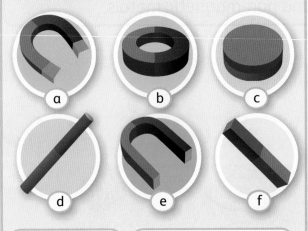

bar magnet	horseshoe magnet
circular magnet	U-shaped magnet
cylindrical magnet	ring magnet

Magnet	Name of magnet
a	
b	
c	
d	
e	
f	

Think like a scientist!

Not all magnets are the same shape or size. Some are round. Some are bar-shaped. Some are shaped liked a ring, or like a horseshoe. Some magnets are stronger than others.

2

This sculpture is made from magnets and magnetic materials. A sculpture is an artwork.

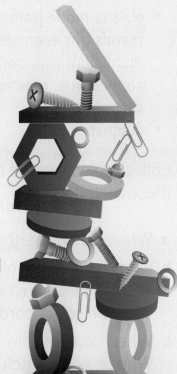

a Make a sculpture using one magnet and magnetic materials.

b Take a photograph or draw a picture of your sculpture. Place it in your Magnet book. Write down how you made it and the objects you used.

c Present your sculpture to the class. Ask the class what they think of it.

Strongest magnet fair test

1

Lami and Kamka did a **fair test**. They put a paperclip at the end of a ruler (with **standard measurements**) at 0 cm. Then they put a magnet at the other end of the ruler. Next, they slowly moved the magnet down the ruler until it attracted the paperclip. Then they read the measurement on the ruler and recorded their results in this table:

Which magnet is the strongest?

Type of magnet	Distance from magnet (cm)
circular	4
cylindrical	2
horseshoe	7
bar	2
ring	5
U-shaped	3

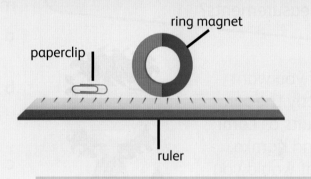

paperclip

ring magnet

ruler

a Lami and Kamka did not finish their work in time. They need your help. Use the results in the table to make a **bar chart**.

b Look at your bar chart. Which magnet is the strongest? Write down your conclusion and use the results to explain why.

c Order the magnets from strongest to weakest.

Scientific words
fair test
standard measurements
bar chart

Why should you use your results in your conclusion?

Testing magnets

Talk partners

On page 77 you read how Lami and Kamka did their fair test. They found out which was the strongest magnet. With a partner, answer these questions.

a How did they make their test fair?

b Why was it important to make their test fair?

c Why did they use standard measurements?

If you want exactly the same results as Lami and Kamka, what would you have to do?

magnetar star

Did you know?

The strongest magnets in the universe are stars called magnetars. Magnetars can destroy small planets if they get close enough!

1

You will need...
- six different magnets
- ruler
- paperclip

Work with a partner to carry out a fair test. Investigate which of your magnets is the strongest.

a Think about what Lami and Kamka did and plan your fair test.

b First, predict which magnet you think will be the strongest. Write down your prediction and why.

c Complete your fair test and record the results.

d When you have finished the test, look at your results. Was your prediction correct?

e Look at your results again. What is the conclusion to your question? Write your conclusion in one sentence. Make sure you use your test result measurements.

f Compare your results with those of Lami and Kamka. Why do you think the results are different?

Adding to my Magnet book

1

You have learnt a lot about magnets so far. Start on a new page in your Magnet book. Write down as many things as you can about magnets. You could also draw pictures and diagrams. If possible, add photographs to your book.

When you write your sentences, use these words:

horseshoe magnet

magnets

ring magnet

bar magnet

silver

attract

iron

strong

gold

nickel

copper

Challenge yourself!

What else can you find out about magnets? Add the information to your book.

2

Now research some interesting facts about magnets. Add them to your Magnet book.

a What is lodestone? Write the answer in your book.

b Find out about a shepherd named Magnes. He discovered magnets in about 2000 BC. Write about the story and draw a picture.

How do we know there is a magnetic field?

Think like a scientist!

So far, you have learnt that:

- A magnet is very special and is made from metal.
- Magnets produce an area of magnetic force, called a magnetic field.
- Magnetic fields are invisible. We cannot see magnetic fields.
- A magnetic force can work at a distance. This means it can work without touching magnetic material.

We cannot see a magnetic field around a magnet. But if we use **iron filings** we can! Iron filings are tiny bits of the metal, iron. Iron is attracted to magnets.

Look at the pattern in the photograph. A magnet has been placed over iron filings.

Wow! What a great pattern. This pattern is called the magnetic field. The iron filings show:

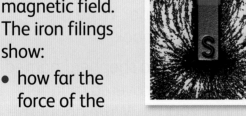

- how far the force of the magnet goes out
- the pattern of the **force field**.

Scientists draw a simpler picture to show the magnetic field like this diagram.

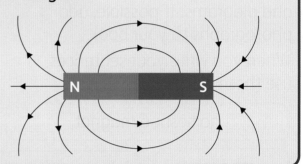

Scientific words

iron filings
force field

Be careful !

Iron filings are very tiny. ALWAYS use them in a sealed container. They can be dangerous if you breathe them in.

1

You will need...

- iron filings sealed in a container
- magnet

Put the magnet underneath the sealed container. Explore what happens to the iron filings.

a What pattern does it make?

b Draw the pattern of the force field. Use a diagram like the one above.

Marvellous magnets

Think like a scientist!

On page 80 you saw that magnets have an invisible magnetic field. We can see the effects of the magnetic field when we use iron filings. Now you will investigate the effects of magnetic fields. Can they work through different materials?

1

You will need...
- collection of materials (such as wood, paper, card, fabrics)
- magnet
- paperclips

Which material does a magnetic field work through? Plan an investigation to find out.

a Predict which materials will allow the magnetic field to work through it.

b Complete your test and write your results in a table, as shown below. Test as many different materials as you like.

c Were all your predictions correct?

d Which predictions were wrong?

e What did you find out? Write your **conclusion**.

Material	Prediction – Will the magnet work through the material?	Was your prediction correct?
felt fabric	*yes*	*no, the felt was too thick for the magnet to work through*
plastic		

Challenge yourself!

Will a magnetic field work through water?

Do magnets work through really thick materials?

Think like a scientist!

Think back to Activity 1 on page 81. A magnetic force can work through different materials. When scientists first explored magnets they wondered: *Can magnets work through really thick materials, or through a thick stack of the same material such as a pile of paper?* What do you think?

Scientific word
equipment

Challenge yourself!

Was your prediction correct?

What other questions can you think of to investigate magnetic forces? Make a list.

1

You will need...
- paperclips
- magnet
- collection of thick materials or a collection of the same materials to make a thick stack

What is the thickest material or stack of the same material that a magnet can work through?

a Talk to a partner and decide on a fair test. Plan your investigation by thinking about these questions:
- *What **equipment** will you need?*
- *What will you change?*
- *What will you keep the same?*
- *What will you measure?*
- *How can you measure using standard measurements such as mm and cm?*
- *How will you record your results?*

b Predict the thickest material or stack of materials that will allow the magnet to work through it.

c Carry out your investigation and record your results.

d Use your results to write your conclusion.

North and south poles

1

Put the ends of the two bar magnets together.

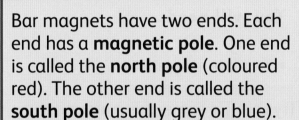

a What happens? What does it feel like?

b Keep swapping ends and putting them together. Does the same thing happen each time?

c Write two sentences to explain what happened.

You will need...
- two bar magnets

Scientific words

magnetic pole
north pole
south pole
repel

Think like a scientist!

Bar magnets have two ends. Each end has a **magnetic pole**. One end is called the **north pole** (coloured red). The other end is called the **south pole** (usually grey or blue).

- What happens if we place the same pole of each magnet together? They will push away from each other. They **repel** each other.

- For example, when we put the south pole of one magnet near the south pole of another magnet, they repel each other. When we put the north pole next to another north pole, the magnets also repel each other.

- When we place the north and south poles near each other, they pull towards each other. They attract each other.

2

Work with a partner. You should have one magnet each.

You will need...
- magnet per person

a Put the ends of your magnets together. What happens? Can you feel an invisible force? In other words, can you feel the magnetic field?

b When do the magnets repel each other? When do magnets attract each other?

c Put the magnets together again and feel the force. Talk about what is happening. Use the words 'attract' or 'repel'.

Poles attract and repel

1

Look at the poles of each pair of magnets. In your mind, put them near each other. Will they attract or repel? Write 'attract' or 'repel' for each pair.

a N   S   N   S   b N   S   S   N

c S   N   S   N   d S   N   N   S

2

a Make up a rhyme, a song or a sentence to help you to remember the rules of the poles. Here is an example of words you could use:

- The same poles together repel each other. North and north or south and south repel each other.

- Opposite poles together attract each other. North and south attract each other.

b Share your rhyme or song with a partner. What does your partner think of it? What do you think of the rhyme or song that your partner made up?

3

You will need...
- string
- two bar magnets

Try this: Tie some string around the middle of a bar magnet. Tie it onto something so that it hangs in the air.

Now make the bar magnet move without touching it. Use another magnet to do this.

This looks like magic!
Ask your partner to try to explain how it works.

What knowledge of magnets will your partner need?

More about north and south poles

1

You will need...

Two of each:
- ring magnet
- horseshoe magnet
- circular magnet

The north and south poles are in different places on different magnets. Look at the three magnets. Where are the poles on each magnet? Explore using two of each magnet. Then draw the magnets and label them to show where the poles are.

 a   b    c

Remember: if the magnets attract, then the touching poles must be north and south. If the poles repel, then the poles must be the same, for example, south and south or north and north.

2

You have learnt a lot about magnets. Start a new page in your Magnet book. Write about and draw all that you can remember about:

a what happens when you put the north and south poles of a magnet together

b a magnet and its magnetic field

c six materials or objects that a magnet's magnetic field can work through.

Challenge yourself!

Use your knowledge of the poles of a ring magnet. Try to make them float on top of each other. Write how you think it works. Use these words to describe what is happening:

- poles
- attract
- repel

How do we use magnets?

Think like a scientist!

Magnets are useful for many things in everyday life. Can you believe that magnets are inside cars, mobile phones, and computers?

Magnets are used in many different ways.
Did you know that in Japan the fast trains use magnets to run on the tracks?

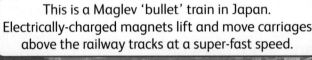
This is a Maglev 'bullet' train in Japan. Electrically-charged magnets lift and move carriages above the railway tracks at a super-fast speed.

1

Look around you to find out where magnets are used. Ask someone at home to help you look. For example, look in cupboards, on fridges and at toys.

Make a list of the things that you find. If you have a camera, take photographs. If possible, print the photographs to put into your Magnet book.

2

Do you have any magnets on your fridge at home?

a Discuss with a partner how a fridge magnet works.

b How would you make a fridge magnet? What would you need?

c Design and make your own fridge magnet. Take it home to put on your fridge.

Magnets are used in recycling rubbish

Think like a scientist!

All over the world, people throw away rubbish. Some rubbish is made from materials that we can recycle. To recycle means to use again. For example, we can recycle glass. Glass is crushed, melted and made into new glass.

Look at the photograph. It shows a machine at a recycling centre sorting rubbish. The machine has a huge magnet that attracts some metals. The magnet separates magnetic metals from other materials. The metals can be melted and used to make new things.

1

Make your own recycling centre.

a Collect small objects made of different materials, for example, cloth, paper, card, plastics, metal spoons and nails.

b Put them in a tray. Then move your strongest magnet over them. This demonstrates how machines sort magnetic metals from other rubbish.

c If you have a camera, take a photograph. Add it to your Magnet book. Then explain how it works. Or, make a video and explain how it works. Show your video to the class. If you cannot do either, draw a picture.

> You need a really strong magnet for this activity!

Challenge yourself!

Look at this picture of a machine in a busy restaurant. The machine has a very strong magnet inside it.

What do you think the magnet will attract?

Magnets can lift cars!

Think like a scientist!

Some magnets are super strong. They can even lift cars!

Scrapyards usually have huge magnets to move cars and metal. A special magnet called an electromagnet is used. The **electromagnet** has an 'on' and 'off' switch. When someone switches the electromagnet on, it picks up metal. It may also move them. When the person switches off the electromagnet switch, it drops the metal onto the ground.

electromagnet picking up metal

1

You will need...

- bar magnet
- cotton
- paperclip
- sticky tape
- clamp stand

Look carefully at the diagram. It shows a paperclip in the air. It looks like magic, but it is really science.

a How do you think it works?

b If you have this equipment, try this.

c If you do not have the clamp stand, what could you use instead?

d Show it to other learners. Explain to them how it works.

S

magnet

clamp stand

N

paperclip

cotton stuck to bench

Scientific word
electromagnet

What could you use instead of a paperclip?

Magnetic games

Think like a scientist!

You have learnt that magnets have many different uses. Sometimes they are used to make children's toys and games. Do you have toys or games that contain magnets? If not, perhaps you have played with toys or games that do?

Challenge yourself!

a This is an interesting way to hang a key. Write a sentence to explain how the key stays in place. Use the scientific words you know.

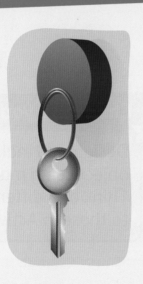

b Look at the handbag. Where do you think a magnet is used? Explain why.

1

Make a magnetic fishing game for younger learners.

a Look carefully at the picture. How do you think the game was made and how do you play it?

b Design your own magnet fishing game. What materials will you need to use? Which part needs to be magnetic? Make your game.

c Let a group of younger learners at school play your game. Make sure you explain how to play the game.

d Did they enjoy it? If you have a camera, take a photograph.

e Put the picture in your 'Magnet book'. Write about how the magnet in the game works.

f Answer these questions: *Why are the fish attracted to the magnet? What metal must the paperclip be made from? Why?*

Useful magnets

1

On page 89 you learnt more ways to use magnets. Now, use magnets to design and make something for others to use. Choose one of these:

- a stick for a physically challenged person, to pick up magnetic objects that she or he cannot reach

- a magnetic pen holder for someone who can never find his or her pen
- something for keeping paperclips together

- a magnetic bookmark for someone who likes reading.

Talk partners

Talk to a partner: How can we use magnets to make a fun game? Share your ideas and then try them. Here is a clue. Think about:

- north pole and south pole
- attract and repel.

Challenge yourself!

Design and make another object using magnets. Think of a different idea to those in Activity 1.

a Draw and annotate your design.

b Make and test it to make sure that it works.

c Think about how you could improve your design.

d Make changes to your design. Retest your design if needed.

e Demonstrate your design to the class.

What have you learnt about magnetism?

1

Write True or False for the following statements.

a Magnets attract all metals.

b Bigger magnets are always stronger than smaller magnets.

c Magnets have two poles, north and south.

d Plastic is attracted to magnets.

e Magnets are not useful.

f Opposite poles attract.

g Two south poles will repel each other.

h Aluminum is a magnetic metal.

i Iron is a magnetic metal.

j Magnets can sometimes work through materials.

k You can see a magnetic field.

What can you remember?

You have been learning about magnetism. Can you:

✔ tell someone three safety rules for using magnets?

✔ name four different kinds of magnets?

✔ name which metals a magnet attracts?

✔ name some materials that are not attracted to a magnet?

✔ describe what happens when you have two magnets and you put the poles close to each other?

✔ explain what the words 'attract' and 'repel' mean?

✔ name things that people use, which have magnets in them?

What do you know about circuit components?

Think like a scientist!

Do you remember making a lamp light up? You did this by making a **circuit**. To make an electrical circuit, you need a **lamp, lamp holder** and **wire**. These are **circuit components**. You also need **cells (battery)**.

When we put two cells together we call them a battery.

cell

battery

Scientific words

circuit
lamp
lamp holder
wire
circuit components
cells (battery)
buzzer

1

A   B   C   D   E   F

a Look at the circuit components in the diagram. Copy this table. Complete it by choosing words from the boxes.

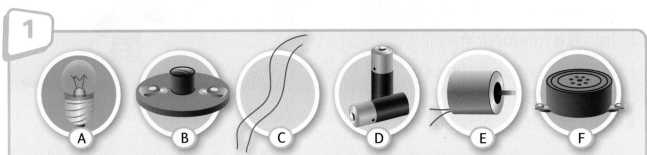

Picture	Name of circuit component
A	
B	
C	
D	
E	
F	

wires   **buzzer**

lamp   motor

cells (battery)   lamp holder

b Use the components to make a circuit. How do you know if your circuit works? What happens if you remove something? What happens if parts of your circuit do not touch properly?

Simple circuits

Think like a scientist!

Remember: A simple circuit is just a cell, lamp, lamp holder and wires. It is not complicated. But sometimes a simple circuit does not work. Think back to when you first learnt about simple circuits. Did they always work?

For a circuit to work, you need a **complete circuit**.
All the **components** must be the right way around.
The components must also all be connected (touching each other).

1

Here are some diagrams of simple circuits.

a Copy each one exactly, using your components.
Which circuits are complete, and will work?
Which circuits do not work?

Scientific words
complete circuit
components

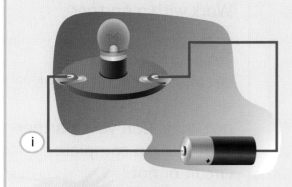

i

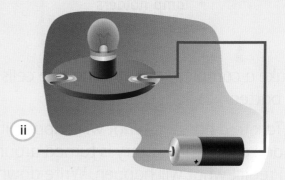

ii

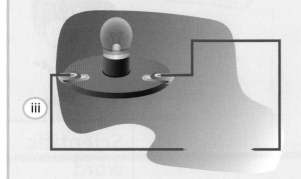

iii

b Copy and complete this table to show your results.

Circuit	Does it work?	Reason
i		
ii		
iii		

Testing circuits

1

You will need...
- two cells (battery)
- lamps
- lamp holders
- wires

Make a complete circuit using two cells (a battery) to light the lamp.

a Talk to a partner. What will happen if one cell in the battery is turned around? Predict what will happen. Write down your prediction.

b Now try it out. Was your prediction right?

c What is your **conclusion**? Does it matter if you turn one of the cells around in a circuit?

d Try making the circuit with a single cell. Are the results the same if you turn the cell around?

Talk partners

Work with a partner. Test each other.

Take turns to make a circuit. The circuit might be correct, or it might not work. Can your partner spot if it is a complete circuit or not?

Scientific word
conclusion

Electrical appliances at home

Think like a scientist!

We use electricity every day – at home, at school and other places. Look at the examples of **electrical appliances**. Electrical appliances use electricity to make them work.

Electricity is made at a **power station**. It travels down large **cables** (wires) to homes and buildings. This electricity is called **mains electricity**. Mains electricity is extremely dangerous. In fact, it can kill. We need to be very careful when using mains electricity.

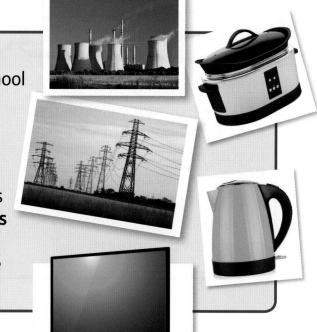

Be careful !

Mains electricity is very useful – if it is used correctly. Read, remember and follow the safety rules. If you do not, you could get an **electric shock**. An electric shock can kill you.

SAFETY RULES
- Do not climb trees or fly kites near power lines.
- Do not put your fingers or anything else in a socket.
- Do not put drinks or **liquids** near electrical appliances.
- Do not use electrical appliances in the bathroom or near water.
- Do not put the plugs of many appliances into one socket.
- Do not pull a plug out of a socket by pulling the wire.

1

Make a mini-book to explain the electricity safety rules to younger learners. Draw pictures or print pictures from the internet to illustrate the book. Remember to add a reason for each rule. When you have finished, share your mini-book with a younger learner.

Scientific words
electrical appliances
power station
cables
mains electricity
electric shock
liquids

Fun with circuits

Think like a scientist!

Lamps use electricity. Cells, or batteries, produce electricity. Cells (batteries) that you use in your investigations are safe. Remember to be careful with mains electricity. Never use mains electricity in your investigations!

2

You will need...
- card
- lamps
- lamp holders
- cells (battery)
- wires
- pencil
- crayons
- scissors

Zaid has made a name card for his desk. How did he light up his name? You will notice that he used lamps.

a Make a light-up name card for your desk.

b Talk to your partner. Share ideas about how Zaid attached the light. Where is the circuit? What does the circuit look like?

c Help each other to make name cards. Which part of your name will you light up?

d Once you have finished, put your name card on your desk. Switch on the light.

1

You will need...
- cells (battery)
- lamps
- wires
- stopwatch, clock or timer

Have a circuit race with a partner.

a Make a complete circuit while a partner times you using the stopwatch. Write down the time.

b Swap and time your partner. Write down the time. Who is quickest?

c Both of you have two more turns. Try to beat your own record.

d What is your average time to complete a circuit?

Remembering circuits

Think like a scientist!

You have learnt these facts about circuits:

- We can use electricity from a single cell or battery to make a lamp light.
- Electricity **flows** around a circuit when there is a complete circuit.
- When there is a complete circuit the lamp will light.
- A gap or break in a circuit is called a **circuit break**.
- Electricity cannot flow if there is a circuit break.
- Electricity cannot flow if parts do not touch properly.

Scientific words

flows

circuit break

equipment

switch

1

You will need...
- two cells (battery)
- wires
- buzzer

Work with a partner to explore how buzzers work.

a Construct a complete circuit to make a buzzer buzz.

b Does it matter which way around the buzzer goes in the circuit?

c How can you stop the buzzer from making a noise?

Talk partners

Use the same **equipment** as in Activity 1. Work with your partner. Use the buzzer to make a pattern of seven buzzes. Use a **switch** to do this.

Ask your partner to listen to your buzzer pattern. Then your partner must copy your pattern using a switch. Swap and repeat.

Motors

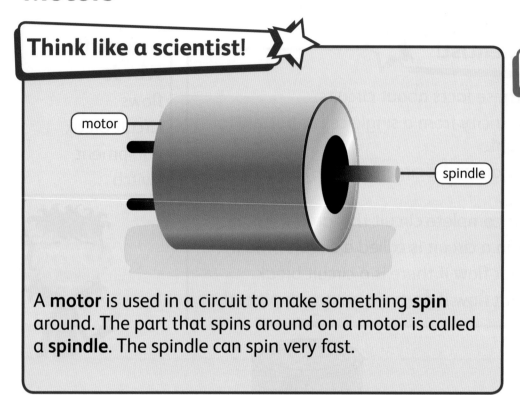

Think like a scientist!

motor

spindle

A **motor** is used in a circuit to make something **spin** around. The part that spins around on a motor is called a **spindle**. The spindle can spin very fast.

Be careful !

To stay safe, NEVER touch the spindle when the motor is on.

Scientific words

motor
spin
spindle

1

You will need...

- two cells (battery)
- wires
- motor
- paper and card
- modelling clay
- scissors, round object to draw around (about 6 cm across)

Put together a circuit to make a motor spin.

a Cut circles from card, about 6 cm across (use a round object). Draw different patterns on each circle.

b Put one circle on the spindle of the motor. Complete the circuit so that the circle spins. Sometimes the circle flies off the spindle. What can you do to solve this problem?

c What happens to the circle? What happens to the pattern on the circle?

d Try out your other circles with patterns. Does the pattern stay the same?

Using circuit components

1

You will need...
- cells (battery)
- wires
- pencils and coloured pens
- paper or thin card
- buzzer
- lamp
- glue
- junk model materials
- motor
- lamp holder

A group of learners made models using circuit components. They used either a lamp, buzzer or motor. Rahel made a robot with a light-up nose.

a Make your own circuit model. It could be a house, an animal or anything else. It must have a circuit component such as a lamp, buzzer or motor.

b Show your circuit model to others in your class. Ask what they think of it. Also ask for a way to improve your circuit model.

c When you have finished, draw a picture of the circuit. What does it look like?

d Which components did you use?

e Where are the wires and which components are they attached to?

Did you know?

a group of wind turbines on a wind farm, used to produce electricity

We can make electricity from the wind – called wind power. We use the Sun for solar power. We use the waves at sea for wave power. We use water for hydroelectric power. We even use animal droppings! This is called biogas energy.

Batteries and cells

 Think like a scientist!

Scientific words

volts

electric current

Some people talk about a battery in a circuit. Other people talk about a cell. A battery is made up of two or more cells.

The V on a cell or battery means **volts**. A battery or cell with '1.5 V' on it means that it has 1.5 volts. Volts tell you the amount of 'push' the cell or battery gives. Push makes the **electric current** move or travel (flow) around the circuit. The more volts, the more push the cell or battery gives.

1

Look at these batteries and cells.

a What do you notice? Write down four things that are similar and four things that are different.

b What kind of cells and batteries do you use in your classroom? Look for your cell or battery in the picture. Can you find it?

c Look again at your cell or battery. You should see a number such as: 1.5 V, 3 V or 4.5 V. What number is on your cell or battery?

2

Look at these cells and batteries. Put them in order – from most 'push' to least 'push' (volts).

Challenge yourself!

Find out the name of the scientist who invented the cell (battery).

a Where did he come from?

b What did the first cell or battery look like?

c What do you notice about his name and 'volt'?

Series circuits

Think like a scientist!

On page 100 you learnt that different cells and batteries have different amounts of 'push' (volts). Push makes the **electricity** flow around the circuit. Now you will learn a new fact for constructing a simple circuit. Check the voltage on the lamp you are using. Make sure that the voltage of the cell or battery is the same. If the cell or battery voltage is higher it might 'blow the lamp'. Then the wire in the lamp will burn out and the lamp will not light.

Look at the simple circuit below. This type of circuit is called a **series circuit**. Follow the circuit with your finger. A series circuit is like a circle. Each component follows, one after the other. It is similar to a television series – one programme follows the other.

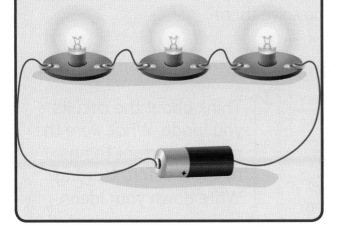

Scientific words
electricity
series circuit
record

1

You will need...
- cells (battery)
- lamp
- wire
- lamp holders

Make a series circuit with one cell so that a lamp lights up.

a Keep adding lamps to the circuit. Find out what happens. First, talk about what you think will happen. Then write down your prediction.

b Copy and complete this table to **record** your results.

Number of lamps	What happens in the circuit?
1	
2	
3	
4	
5	

c What did you find out about adding lamps to a circuit with only one cell?

d You want all the lamps in your circuit to light. What must you do to make this happen? Test your idea. Did it work?

Using a series circuit

Think like a scientist!

On page 101 you kept adding lamps to create a series circuit. The more lamps you added, the dimmer the lamps became. If you add a motor to the circuit on page 101 it will not work. This is because a single 1.5 V cell does not have enough voltage (push) to light the lamps and run the motor at the same time. But, if you add another cell to the circuit to make a battery, then all the components should work!

1

You will need...

- card
- cells (battery)
- wires
- lamps
- lamp holders
- motor
- pencils and coloured pens

Think about what you have learnt about series circuits. Use lights and a motor to make a whizzy picture. Zara made a clown: On the clown's face, the eyes light up and a motor makes the bow tie spin around.

a Make your own picture of a clown: by using a series circuit, its eyes should light and the bow tie should spin around.

b Did you have any problems? How did you solve them? Copy and complete this table.

My problem	How I solved the problem

c Show your picture to other learners. Ask what they think. Talk about any problems you had. How did you solve them?

Challenge yourself!

Think about the circuits you made. What were the most important things to know before starting? Write down your ideas.

What happens to electricity in a circuit?

Think like a scientist!

You have made circuits that make lamps light, buzzers sound and motors spin. You could not see the electricity that made them work. But, you saw the effect that the electricity had to make the things happen.

Now you will find out how electricity works in a circuit.

1

You will need...
- cells (battery)
- lamp
- lamp holder
- wires

Think about what you know about circuits.

a Make a complete circuit so that the lamp lights.

b What happens to the electricity in the circuit? Talk to a partner and share your ideas.

c Now draw the circuit. Show what you think happens to the electricity.

Hint:
Use arrows to show the flow of electricity. Or, add a title or explanation in a sentence to your drawing.

Electrical current flow model

Think like a scientist!

Scientific words
flow of particles
models

Electrical current, or electricity, is sometimes difficult to understand. This is because we cannot see it. We can only see the effects of electricity. Examples are when lamps light and buzzers buzz.

Electricity is the **flow of particles** around a circuit. We cannot see the particles. But this does not mean that the particles are not there.

Scientists sometimes use **models** to help them to explain things. We cannot see electricity flowing in a circuit. So, we need to use a model. Your model will help you to understand how electricity flows in a circuit. You will be able to describe how particles travel around a circuit.

1

You will need...

- group of six learners
- head band that says 'cell'
- head band that says 'lamp'
- diagram of a circuit

Look at the picture. The learners are modelling a circuit. They are pretending to be a complete series circuit. One learner is wearing a hat that says 'lamp'. Another learner's hat says 'cell'.

- When everyone is holding hands the circuit is complete. The 'cell' must shout 'electricity' and then squeeze the hand of the person to the right. Then that person must pass on the squeeze around the circle.

- The squeeze represents electricity flowing around the circuit.

- Carry on until the electricity (squeeze) reaches the 'lamp'. That person must shout 'light'. Then keep the electricity flowing.

Try this circuit model with your group.

⏻ Breaking the electrical flow

1

On page 104 you modelled a complete series circuit. You will use that model again. Now you will see what happens when there is a break in a circuit.

a Repeat what you did on page 104. This time one person in the circuit should not hold hands. That person creates a break in the circuit.

b What happens to the flow of electricity when the circuit breaks?

c When the circuit breaks, what happens to the lamp? Will it light?

d Share your ideas with the rest of the group.

Challenge yourself!

Humphry Davy was an English scientist. In the year 1800, he made the first electric light. Imagine that you are Humphry Davy. You have just made the first light. How do you think Davy felt? What might he have said? Create a one-minute play with a partner. The play should be about the first time an electric light was lit. Perform your play for the class.

 Switches

Think like a scientist!

On pages 104 and 105 your group modelled two different circuits. You learnt that if a circuit is not complete, there is a break in the circuit. This is a circuit break, and electricity cannot flow.

Sometimes we want to add circuit breaks on purpose. Circuit breaks allow us to turn a light or other component on and off. Something that turns a light on and off is called a switch. Electrical appliances are devices that have switches. We need to be able to turn the switches on and off. You may have many switches at school or at home.

light switch

Did you know?

Electricity travels at the speed of light – that is 299,792 kilometres per second. That is super-fast!

1

You will need...
- cells (battery) • wires • lamp
- lamp holder

Work with a partner and make a circuit to light a lamp.

a Predict what will happen: if you break the circuit by taking a wire off the cell.

b What did happen? Was your prediction right?

c Why do you think the circuit does not work when there is a break?

Hint:
What happens to the electricity in your circuit when there is a break?

d Talk about what you have learnt about circuit breaks. What happens when there is a circuit break?

e Repeat the activity to see how many ways you can break the circuit. Draw pictures to show the different ways.

Looking for switches

Think like a scientist!

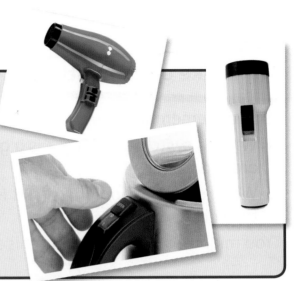

Electrical appliances work using circuits and switches. Circuits allow electricity to flow so that lamps light, motors move and buzzers buzz.

A switch is used to complete or break a circuit. Switches allow us to turn lights, motors or buzzers on or off.

1

With a partner, look around your classroom or school. How many different switches can you find?

a Draw each switch or take a photograph. Look at different appliances and light switches.

b Write down the number of switches you found.

c Sort the switches into groups. How will you label each group?

d Share what you have found with another pair. Show them how you have grouped your switches. What do they think of your sorting groups?

Be careful !

Remember: Do not touch switches without permission.
Never put anything into switches.
Never touch them with wet hands.
Switches that are connected to mains electricity can be dangerous and hurt you if you do not use them properly.

Talk partners

Work with a partner. Think of reasons why switches are useful. Make a list. Share your list with another pair in your class. What is on their list that is different to yours?

Did you know?

Electric eels can produce electric shocks. They do this for self-defence and for hunting food. Do you think electric eels have switches to turn the electricity on and off?

How switches work

Think like a scientist!

Do you remember how a switch works? Here is a reminder:

- When a switch is off, there is a gap in the circuit. Electricity cannot flow around the circuit.
- When a switch is on, the circuit is complete. Electricity can flow around the circuit.

You might remember making this switch in Stage 2.

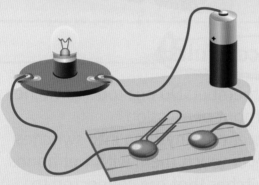

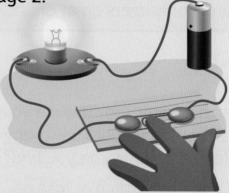

This diagram shows a break in the circuit. The electricity cannot go around the circuit. The switch is off.

Here there is no break in the circuit. The electricity can go around the circuit. The switch is on.

Challenge yourself!

You will need...
- two drawing pins
- sticky tape
- balsa wood or card
- lamp
- lamp holder
- screwdriver
- paperclips
- cell
- wires

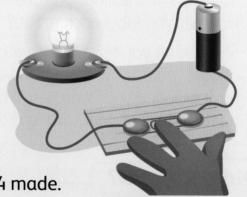

a Look at this picture of a switch that Class 4 made.

b Now make this switch to turn the lamp on and off in a circuit.

c If you can, take a photograph of your circuit. If not, draw your circuit.

d Does it matter where the switch is in your circuit? Write a conclusion.

Different switches

Think like a scientist!

On page 108 you made a simple switch. There are many types of switches. Examples are push-button switches, slide switches and toggle switches. They all work by making a gap in the circuit – to break the flow of electricity. Then they close the gap – so there is no break in the flow of electricity.

Talk partners

Talk to a partner about how each switch works. What do you think happens inside each switch?

push-button switch · slide switch · toggle switch

1

Hamida made a model of a car. Hamida found a switch, which she used to make headlights that switch on and off.

a Design and make your own model car.

b Use a switch to make the headlights go on and off.

c Add a buzzer so that you can sound the horn.

d What will you do if the circuit does not work?

e Make sure that no-one can see the circuit inside your model. How will you hide it?

f If possible, photograph your model car while it is working.

You will need...
- cells (battery)
- lamps
- lamp holders
- switch • wires
- buzzer
- boxes for modelling
- glue or sticky tape
- coloured pens

Making a model

Think like a scientist!

There are many fun ways to use what you know about circuits and switches. Look at what other learners have made.

a working light in a doll's house

a fairground ride that goes around

a birthday card that lights up

- What is working in each circuit?
- What do you think each circuit looks like?
- What does the switch in each circuit do?

1

Choose one thing above to make. Use what you know about circuits and switches. When you have finished, show your partner how it works.

You will need...
- wires
- lamps
- motors
- lamp holders
- card
- glue
- coloured pens
- cells (batteries)

Question and answer circuit board

1

Some learners made a 'question and answer' board using circuit components. A lamp lights when an answer is correct because the circuit is complete. The questions are for young learners and are about animals. These diagrams show how the board works.

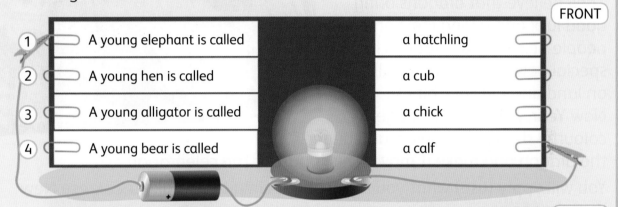

FRONT

1. A young elephant is called — a hatchling
2. A young hen is called — a cub
3. A young alligator is called — a chick
4. A young bear is called — a calf

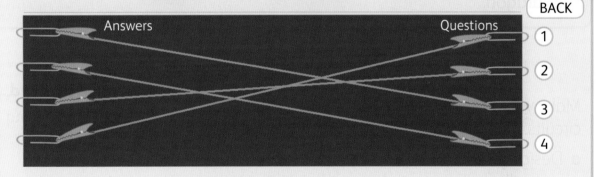

BACK

Answers   Questions
1
2
3
4

You will need...
- piece of card
- wires
- lamp and lamp holder
- metal paperclips or paper fasteners (split pins)
- paper
- scissors
- glue
- crocodile clips

a Work with a partner to make a 'question and answer' board. What kinds of questions will you use? Make sure you know the correct answers.

b Draw a plan of your board.

c Collect the components that you will need to make your board.

d Make your board and check that it works.

e Give it to others to try out. Ask how they think your board could be improved.

Make a Chinese New Year dragon

Think like a scientist!

Have you ever seen a Chinese New Year dragon? Dragons are important to Chinese people. They believe that dragons bring good luck and a long life. Some people believe that dragons have special powers. They can walk on land and fly! For Chinese New Year, people make huge colourful dragons. People stand under the dragon and make it move. This is part of the celebration.

You will apply (use) what you know about circuits to make a Chinese New Year dragon.

1

Make your dragon using what you know about series circuits:

a Design your dragon. Draw a plan of the circuits you will use. For example:

- Give the dragon eyes that light up.
- Use a motor to make something on the dragon spin around.
- Use a switch to make the eyes flash and turn on and off.

b Make your dragon. How will you hide the circuit components? No-one should be able to see them.

c Complete your dragon. Demonstrate it to the rest of the class.

d Explain how the electricity flows through your series circuit to make the lamps, motor and switch work.

You will need...

- junk modelling materials
- lamp
- lamp holder
- wire • switch
- motor
- cells (batteries)

What have you learnt about electricity?

1

Make a mind map. Write down and draw everything you have learnt about electricity and circuits. Make sure you use the words below. Also use other words you can think of.

series circuit	lamp	cell	switch	volts
mains electricity	motor	buzzer	appliances	spindle
flow of particles	battery	circuit	break	current

2

Write True or False for each of these sentences.

a A series circuit has only one bulb.

b A switch breaks the current of electricity flowing around a circuit.

c The voltage shows the weight of the cell or battery.

d A battery is two or more cells put together.

e Electrical appliances do not have circuits inside them.

f Mains electricity can kill you.

g The wind can make electricity.

What can you remember?

You have been learning about making circuits. Can you:

✔ construct a complete circuit to make a lamp light?

✔ tell someone rules about mains electricity safety?

✔ explain what happens where there is a break in a circuit?

✔ explain how electrical current (electricity) flows in a circuit?

✔ show, using a model, how particles travel around a circuit?

✔ describe how a switch in a circuit works?

✔ describe a series circuit?

What do you already know about sound?

1

Sound is all around us. Raindrops splash. The wind whistles. Birds chirp. Mice squeak. Babies cry. We talk and sing. These are just a few examples of everyday sounds. You probably know more about **sound** and its **sources** than you think!

a Make a **mind map**. Draw and write what you know about sound.

b Use as many of these words as you can in your mind map:

sound	source	fainter	**loud**
quiet	noisy	noise	ear
travel	whisper	**soft**

2

Remember: Things that make sounds are called **sources of sound**.

a Talk about things you can **hear**. What makes the sounds (the sources of sound) in different places?

b Copy and complete this table.

Sources of sound at home	Sources of sound outdoors	Sources of sound at school

Scientific words

| sound | sources | mind map | loud |
| soft | sources of sound | | hear |

I think, if you walk away from a sound, the sound will get fainter. — Damola

I think the sound will stay the same. — Jari

I think the sound will get louder if you walk away from it. — Lekie

Talk partners

a Who do you think is right? Explain why to a partner.

b How can you prove that you are right? What can you do?

c Try your idea. Are you right?

d Talk to another pair. Share what you did and what you found out.

Animal ears

Think like a scientist!

Whatever is making a sound is called the source of the sound. Imagine that you hear a cat meowing. The cat is the source of the sound.

What do you know about **ears**? We hear with our ears. Animals also use their ears to hear. Animal ears are different shapes. The shapes depend on where they live and what they eat.

Predators are animals that eat other animals. Predators have ears that face forward because this focuses the sound as they stalk their **prey**. Prey is food for animals. Look at these predators' ears.

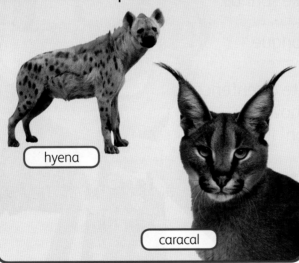

hyena

caracal

Some prey animals have ears that swivel (move), so that they can hear predators more easily!

1

a Look at the different animals below. Where are the ears on each animal? If you do not know, do some research to find out.

owl

desert fox

cobra

elephant

giraffe

tortoise

b Your ears are at the side of your head. Look at the desert fox. Why are its ears so large? Why do the ears face forwards? Write down your answers.

Scientific words

ears

predators

prey

How are sounds made?

Think like a scientist!

Sounds are made when objects **vibrate**. Vibrate means to move backwards and forwards very fast. When you clap your hands, your hands vibrate. This makes the air around your hands vibrate. The **vibrations** enter your ear and you hear the sound.

We can see some vibrations – such as when you twang a plastic ruler. (Look at the picture on the next page.) We can feel some vibrations – put your hand on your throat and hum. We cannot see some vibrations but we can hear a sound. In this case, something must be vibrating for the sound to be made.

1

Put your fingers on your **voice box** and speak. Can you feel your voice box vibrate? When your voice box vibrates, it vibrates the air around. The vibrations enter the ear and you can hear the sound of your voice.

a Now use these parts of the body to make sounds:

hands   feet   fingers   tongue

b Think about how you make sounds. Write a sentence for each part of the body and describe how you made the sound. Use the word 'vibration' in each sentence.

Scientific words
vibrate
vibrations
voice box

Be careful

Do not press too hard on your voice box!

Feeling and seeing vibrations

Think like a scientist!

We cannot see sound but we can hear it. We cannot see air vibrating. We can see or feel the source of the sound vibration. You will now do some activities to help you understand sound. When an object vibrates, it makes a sound.

1

Use a plastic ruler to investigate vibrations.

Be careful ⚠

Do not let go of the ruler!
Do not break the ruler.

a When you flick the ruler on the edge of a table, what happens? Write a sentence using these words:

flick | ruler | sound | vibration

b What happens to the sound when you do these things?

i Flick the ruler gently and make a small vibration.

ii Flick the ruler very hard and make a big vibration.

flicking a ruler on the edge of a table

Write a sentence to describe what happens. Use these words:

sound | vibration | small | big | loud | soft

2

You will need...
- tuning fork
- plastic cup
- water

Work with a partner. Fill a plastic cup nearly to the top with water. Tap the tuning fork on the table. Do this until it vibrates and makes a sound. Then put it in the water. What happens?

a Talk to your partner about the sound that the tuning fork makes.

b Why does the water splash out of the cup?

Drum investigation

Think like a scientist!

In Activity 1 on page 117 you saw the ruler vibrate. You also heard the sound it made. You tapped the tuning fork on the table. It probably made a humming sound. You saw the water splash out of the cup. This was because the tuning fork was vibrating. Here are more activities to help you understand sound and vibrations. This time you will use a drum.

Be careful

Never make loud sounds next to someone's ears! You could damage their hearing.

1

You will need...
- drum
- drum stick

a Work with a partner. Your partner will place a hand just above the drum skin. You tap the drum. (Do not hit your partner's hand!)

b Swap and try the activity again. Tell each other what you felt. Use the word 'vibrate'.

2

You will need...
- rice (or seeds)
- drum
- drum stick

This is a good activity to do outside on grass. This way, no-one will slip on the rice (or seeds).

a Put some rice on the drum. Tap the drum. What happens?

b Why does the rice jump? How does this link to sound and vibrations? Tell your partner.

c Explore different sounds. Tap the drum in different ways and on different parts. What happens?

d Describe to your partner what you discovered. Discuss the drum and how you made the sounds.

e Draw a diagram showing how a drum makes sounds. Annotate (label) your diagram.

How sound travels

Think like a scientist!

On page 118 you felt the drum vibrate when you tapped it. You also saw the seeds or rice jump off the drum skin. This happened because the drum skin was vibrating.

Remember that when something vibrates the air around it vibrates. The tiny **air particles** vibrate and knock against each other, passing the vibration to your ear. Your brain works out what the sound is.

1

Read the 'Think like a scientist' box again. Imagine that you are an air particle above the drum.

a What do you think happens to you (as an air particle) when someone hits the drum? Draw and label a diagram to show this.

b Now write a sentence to describe this. Try to use some of these words:

| air particles | vibrate | hit |
| drum skin | knock | sound |

2

Work with a partner. Find and inflate (blow up) a balloon.

a Hold the inflated balloon between you. Talk onto your side of the balloon. The other side of the balloon should be against your partner's ear. What does your partner feel and hear? Swap places.

b What is happening to the air particles in the balloon? What is vibrating?

c Draw and annotate (label) a picture showing what you did and what you found out.

Scientific word
air particles

 Drumming

Think like a scientist!

You have been exploring how sounds are made. When objects vibrate, the air around them vibrates. The vibrations pass to your ear. Now you will use what you know to make percussion instruments. These instruments make sounds when you hit or shake them.

1

a Look carefully at the drums from around the world. How do you think they are made?

b Design and make your own drum. First draw a plan. What resources will you use?

c Make your drum. Then use it to create some music.

bodhran · ashiko · dunun · goblet drum · djembe · bongos · talking drum

d How can you change the sound that your drum makes? What can you do to make the drum louder or softer?

e Play your drum to the class. Explain how a drum makes sounds. Use the 'sound' words that you know so far:

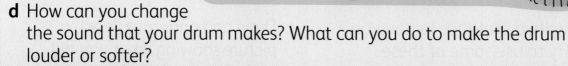

vibration · travel · vibrate · air · particles · sound · source · hear · ear

f In groups, listen to drumming music from around the world. You might find some on the internet. Then have your own drumming session.

Louder and softer

Think like a scientist!

In the activity on page 120 you made a drum. You learnt that hitting the drum harder made a louder sound. Hitting the drum gently made a softer sound. When an object makes a big vibration the sound is louder. When the object makes a small vibration the sound is softer.

1

Think back to when you put your hand on your voice box.
You felt it vibrate.

a Do this again. This time, change your voice. Make it loud and then soft. Then make it loud and then soft again.

b What do you notice about the different vibrations?

c Write two sentences about what you can feel. Begin with:

- The louder the sound _____
- The softer the sound _____

2

Think back to Activity 2 (page 118). You put rice on a drum, which you hit. The rice flew into the air.

a Do this investigation again. This time, hit the drum hard. Then hit it more gently.

b What happens to the rice? What does this tell you about the vibrations?

c Copy and complete these sentences using these words:

[softer] [louder]

- The bigger the vibration, the _____ the sound.
- The smaller the vibration, the _____ the sound.

How sounds are made

Think like a scientist!

Sounds are made when objects vibrate. Air particles vibrate. The vibrations pass to your ear so that you can hear. Materials also vibrate. Different materials make different sounds. You can make a sound louder by making the vibration bigger. If the vibration is smaller the sound is softer.

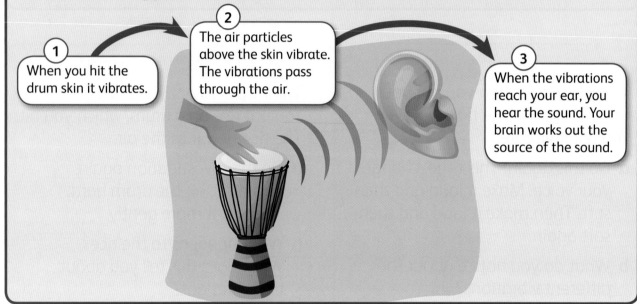

1 When you hit the drum skin it vibrates.

2 The air particles above the skin vibrate. The vibrations pass through the air.

3 When the vibrations reach your ear, you hear the sound. Your brain works out the source of the sound.

1

Look back at your mind map from page114. Look at what you drew and wrote about sound.

a Since then, what else have you learnt about sound? Add the information to your mind map. Use a different-coloured pen or pencil.

b Add anything else that you may have learnt.
Check how many of these words you have used:

sound   ears   hear   vibrate   vibration   loud   soft   bigger   smaller

shake   hit   percussion   drum   ruler   tuning fork   balloon   seeds

c Add the words you have not used to your mind map. Give a short explanation for each word.

Measuring sound

Think like a scientist!

How loud or soft a sound is, is called its **volume**. Volume is measured in decibels. We write **decibels** as **dB**.

A **sound level meter** measures the volume of sounds. The louder the sound, the more decibels the meter measures. Very loud sounds can damage ears and hearing. Very loud sounds can also cause **deafness** – make you **deaf**.

1

Think about these sounds:
- someone whispering
- an airplane taking off
- a pneumatic drill going through concrete
- leaves rustling
- a car starting.

Work in pairs.

a Which sounds have you heard?

b How loud were the sounds?

c Put the sounds in order from softest to loudest.

Scientific words
volume
decibels   dB
sound level meter
deafness
deaf

2

Look at the decibel chart below.
Compare it to your list.

a Did you get the order from softest to loudest right?

Source of sound	Decibels (dB)	Volume
leaves rustling	10	soft
watch ticking	20	soft
someone whispering	30	soft
refrigerator	50	loud
car starting	70	loud
hairdryer	90	loud
pneumatic drill	100	painful; can damage hearing; need ear defenders
plane taking off	120	painful; can damage hearing; need ear defenders
space rocket launching	180	will make you deaf; you should not be near it

b Which is louder – a pneumatic drill or a car?

c How many decibels is a watch ticking?

d Imagine a plane taking off. Would it harm your hearing if you stood near it? Explain your answer.

⏻ Reading sound on a meter

Think like a scientist!

Look at the picture of the sound level meter.
As you know, we use a sound level meter to measure
the volume of sound. We measure sound in decibels.
The number on this sound level meter is 90 dB – or
90 decibels. Refer to the decibel table on page 123.
What sound would have been 90 dB of noise?

1

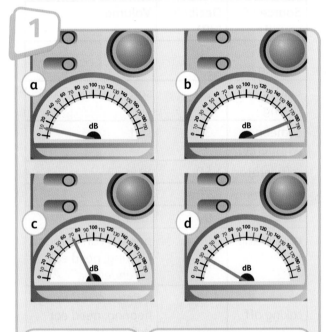

a   b   c   d

| leaves rustling | someone whispering |
| space rocket launching | car starting |

Match each decibel reading to the
source of the sound.

Hint: Use the
decibel table on
page 123 for help.

2

a Talk to a partner. Discuss each
source of sound in this table.
Decide how loud each sound
could be, in decibels.

Source of sound	Decibels (dB)
cat meowing	
learner shouting	
motorbike	
helicopter taking off	
paper rustling	

It will help if you ask these
questions: *Are the sounds similar
to those in the decibel table?
Are they louder?
Are they softer?*

b Copy and complete
the table above.

Classroom sounds

Think like a scientist!

We use a sound level meter to measure sound in decibels (dB). A school in India used a **data logger** to measure the level of sound learners made in class during one day. They used a **line graph** to track the noise level – from the time learners arrived at school until they went home.

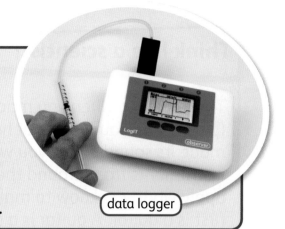
data logger

1

Study the line graph of sound levels of the class. The graph shows how loud and how quiet the learners were at different times of the day.

Use the information to answer the questions.

a What time of day were the learners quietest? How do you know?

b How many decibels were the learners at their loudest?

c What could have happened in class just before lunchtime? Why?

d What time were the learners doing silent reading?

e When did the class clap for Jai for her birthday?

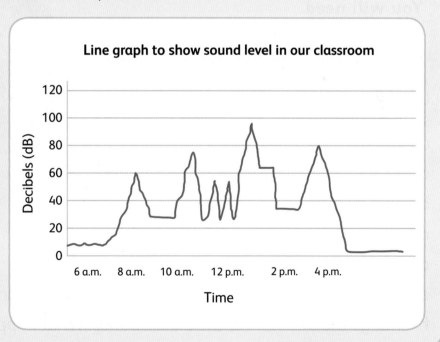

Line graph to show sound level in our classroom

Decibels (dB): 0, 20, 40, 60, 80, 100, 120

Time: 6 a.m., 8 a.m., 10 a.m., 12 p.m., 2 p.m., 4 p.m.

Scientific words
data logger
line graph

Musical instruments around the world

Think like a scientist!

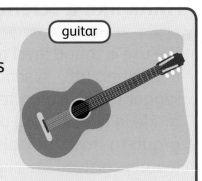

guitar

Think back to when you made percussion instruments (page 120). You found out how each instrument made its sounds. Now you will learn about musical instruments from around the world. Then you will apply what you know to make an instrument – the first is a guitar. A guitar is a stringed instrument.

How does a guitar work? Vibrations create sounds. A guitar makes sounds when someone plucks (pulls or picks up) the strings. The strings vibrate.

1

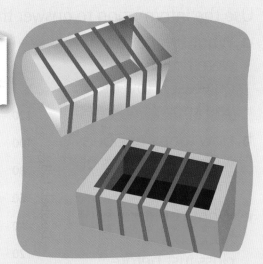

You will need...
- box or tin tray or plastic container
- elastic bands of different sizes and thicknesses

Look at the pictures. Then make your own simple guitar. Explore your guitar to find the answers to these questions.

a How do you make sounds on your guitar?

b What vibrates?

c How do you make the sound louder?

d How do you make the sound softer?

e How can you change the sound? How many ways can you find to do this?

f Change the thickness of the elastic bands. What happens to the sound?

g Make the elastic bands tighter. What happens to the sound?

h Draw a picture of your elastic-band guitar. Add labels to show how to make the sound. If possible, photograph your elastic-band guitar. Write captions around your picture or photograph.

Volume and pitch in stringed instruments

Think like a scientist!

Sounds can be loud or soft – this is called volume.

You changed the thickness of the elastic bands on your guitar. You also changed the tightness of the elastic bands. You probably noticed that the sounds changed. Some sounds were higher and some were lower.

Musicians change sounds to make them lower or higher. We call this changing the **pitch** of a sound. The pitch of a sound is how **high** or **low** a sound is.

Talk partners

Work with a partner. Use your guitars to make loud sounds and soft sounds. Discuss what you did to the elastic bands to make the different sounds.

a Write a sentence to describe what you did to make a soft sound.

b Write a sentence to describe how you made a loud sound. Now use your guitars to make high sounds and low sounds. Discuss what you did to the elastic bands to make the different sounds.

c Write a sentence to describe how you made a high sound.

d Write a sentence to describe how you made a low sound.

the world's smallest guitar magnified

10 microns

Did you know?

The biggest guitar is 13.26 metres long. Is that longer or shorter than a car?

The smallest guitar is only 10 microns long. Ten microns is one-fifth as wide as one hair on your head. Wow!

Scientific words
pitch
high

Volume and pitch in wind instruments

Think like a scientist!

So far you have found that:
- In a drum, the skin vibrates to make a sound.
- In a guitar, the string vibrates to make a sound.

In a musical instrument such as a recorder, the air vibrates to make a sound. We need to make the air in some instruments vibrate to make them work. We call these **wind instruments**.

Look at the picture. Notice that each bottle contains a different amount of water. Anna is blowing across the bottles. The water and the air are vibrating in each bottle. The amount of air in each bottle is called the **column of air**. When Anna blows over each bottle, the column of air vibrates and makes a sound.

Different amounts of water in each bottle make the column of air longer or shorter.

1

You will need...
- some glass bottles

Be careful
Be very careful when using glass!

Make some musical bottles. Set up your musical bottles as you can see in the picture. Blow over them to make sounds.

Remember: The column of air vibrating in the bottle is what makes the sound.

a Explore your musical bottles. How can you change the volume of the sounds?

b What happens as you blow over the bottles? Start at the bottle with the most water. Work through to the bottle with the least water.

c How do you change the pitch of the sounds?

recorder

Scientific words
wind instruments
column of air

Making pan pipes

Think like a scientist!

On page 128 you found out that:

- Blowing over bottles makes a sound.
- Blowing hard over bottles makes the sound louder.
- Blowing softly over bottles makes the sound softer.
- The longer the column of air in the bottle, the lower the pitch.
- The shorter the column of air in the bottle, the higher the pitch.

Pan pipes are a wind instrument. They are made from a row of pipes of different lengths. The pipes are fixed together. To play pan pipes, blow across the tops of the pipes – as you did with the musical bottles. People in Peru played pan pipes 5000 years ago! Today, many people still play pan pipes.

1

You will need...
- eight straws • ruler • card
- sticky tape • scissors

Make your own pan pipes.

a Cut your straws to these lengths: 4 cm, 6 cm, 8 cm, 10 cm, 14 cm, 16 cm, 18 cm and 20 cm.

b Line up your straws from shortest to longest. Put sticky tape across the straws to keep them together.

c On both sides of the straws, place a piece of card. This will make a pipe sandwich.

d Play your pan pipes.

e How can you change the volume of the sound?

f What must you do to play a higher or lower sound?

g Make up a tune by changing the volume and pitch.

h Play your tune to someone else. Explain how you change sounds. Use these words:

column of air | volume | air

pitch | vibrate

How sound travels through different materials

1

You will need...
- string
- metal spoon
- table

a Make a spoon gong.

- Look at the picture. Tie a piece of string to the spoon.

- Hold the end of the string against your ears. Carefully swing the spoon so that it taps against the table. Try different lengths of string.

b What can you hear?

c What does it sound like?

d Work with a partner. Describe how the sound travels to your ears. Use these words to write your sentence:

| string | vibrates | spoon | metal |

| ears | travels | hit |

Think like a scientist!

Think about some sounds that you hear outside. Examples could be birds singing or cars driving past.

How do you think the sound reaches you? Share your ideas with your partner.

Do you think sound can travel through **gas** (air), **solids** and **liquids**? How do you know?

2

a Try the investigation with wooden or plastic spoons. What other materials could you try? What differences do you hear?

b Think about how to **record** what you tried and what happened. Use these words:

| string | vibrates | material | ears |

Challenge yourself!

You know that sound travels through air (a gas). Can sound travel through a solid? How could you test this?

Scientific words

| gas | solids |
| liquids | record |

Can sound travel through water?

1

You will need...
- bowl, half-full of water
- plastic bottle with no lid (end cut off)
- two spoons

Think like a scientist!

Sound can travel through air and solids (such as wood and fabric). But, can sound travel through water (a liquid)? Try these activities to find out.

Work in pairs.

a Ask your partner to tap the two spoons together. Listen carefully. Talk about how the sound gets to your ears.

b Now put the cut end of the plastic bottle carefully into the bowl of water. Put your ear next to the top of the bottle (a solid). Ask your partner to tap the spoons together underwater. What do you hear?

c Swap with your partner and do the same again.

d Talk to your partner about what you both heard. Discuss how the sound got from the spoons to your ears.

e What is your **conclusion**? Can sound travel through water? How could you prove this to someone?

2

You will need...
- bowl, half-full of water
- plastic bottle with no lid (end cut off)
- hard waterproof objects

a Repeat Activity 1. Use different materials such as plastic or wood.

b Predict what will happen when you tap objects underwater. Write down your prediction.

c Do your tests. Was your prediction right?

d What do your tests prove about sound travelling through different materials? Write a sentence using these words:

sound	travel	water
vibrations	air	ear

Scientific word
conclusion

String telephones

1

You will need...
- piece of string 15 m long
- two plastic cups
- pencil
- paperclip

a Work in pairs to make
a string telephone.

- Use a pencil to make
a hole at the bottom of each plastic cup.

- Thread the string through each cup. Make a knot. Push the paperclip
through the knot.

- The paperclip will stop the string from sliding out of the cup.

- You are now ready to explore using your string telephone. Make sure you
find a place with enough room for you to work.

b Draw a picture of you and your partner using the string telephone.
Explain how the sound travels from you to your partner. Use speech bubbles.
In your sentences, use these words:

| string | voice | passed | ear | cup | vibration | along |

Talk partners Talk to a partner. Change the design of your telephone.
Think of a question, for example: *Does having more strings
make the sound louder?* Ideas of things you could change:
number of strings, length, type of material, three, four or
five cups.

Make sure you find out the answer to your question.

 Stopping sounds

Think like a scientist!

Sometimes people do not want sound to reach their ears. The table on page 123 listed the sound level of a pneumatic drill as 100 dB. This is so loud that it can damage your hearing. It might even make you go deaf. An aircraft taking off is even louder – 120 dB. This sound can make you go deaf very quickly. The big sound vibrations can damage your ears.

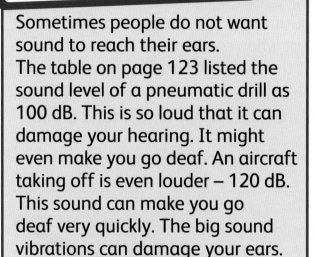

The person in the photograph is using **ear defenders**. Ear defenders protect the ears and prevent damage to hearing.

Scientific words
ear defenders
bar chart

1

You will need...
- ticking clock or radio
- different materials (fabric, cotton wool, bubble wrap, paper)
- sound level meter

a Investigate to find the best material for making ear defenders. Plan a fair test. Think about:
- How will you test the materials?
- What will you do?
- What will you change?
- How will you make your test fair? (What will you keep the same?)
- What will you measure?

b Before doing the test, make a prediction: Which material will be best for making ear defenders? Write down your prediction.

c Test each material. Copy this table and record your results.

Material	dB (decibels)
fabric	
cotton wool	
bubble wrap	
paper	

d Use your table to make a **bar chart**. What is your conclusion?

Make a new musical instrument

Think like a scientist!

You have learnt how to make different instruments. You made percussion, string and wind instruments. You learnt that when something vibrates, the instrument makes a sound. You also learnt that you can change the volume and pitch of the sound of each instrument.

Now you will apply what you know to make a musical instrument for a band. Then you will perform a song for your class.

1

Here are some ideas of instruments you could make.

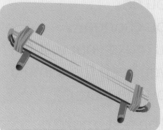

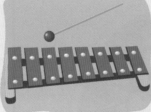

This is a lolly-stick kazoo. To make a sound, you blow between the lolly sticks.

This is a whirling drum. It is a small drum that you hold it in your hand. People in China and Japan play this drum.

This is a xylophone. You tap it to make sounds.

This is a rainmaker. People in countries such as Peru and Africa use this instrument. It is called a rainmaker because it makes a sound like rain falling. It is made from a tube filled with seeds. A rainmaker is a percussion instrument.

Work in a group. Discuss the instruments your band will use.

a Decide which instrument you will each make. Will it be a percussion, string or wind instrument? Make sure you have a balance of different instruments.

b Work alone to draw a plan of your instrument. Write down how your instrument will make its sound. What vibrates? Label this on your drawing.

c Make your instrument. Practise playing it. If necessary, adjust your instrument. You need to be able to change the volume and pitch.

d With your group, create and practise a piece of music. Perform it for the class. Demonstrate how your instruments can change volume and pitch.

What have you learnt about sound?

1

Think back to the beginning of this unit when you started a mind map about sound.

a Look at your mind map. Think about everything that you now know about sound. What else can you add to your mind map? Add anything new in a different-coloured pen or pencil.

b Compare what you wrote at the beginning to what you know now.

What is the most important thing you learnt about sound?

What can you remember?

You have been learning about sound. Can you:

✔ explain how sounds are made when objects, materials or air vibrate?

✔ describe what 'volume' means?

✔ use a sound level meter to measure the volume of sound in decibels?

✔ say what equipment is used to measure sound?

✔ say how sound travels through different materials to the ear?

✔ describe how to test which materials are good at preventing sound from travelling through them?

✔ explain what 'pitch' is?

✔ describe high and low sounds and say why they can be loud or soft?

✔ explain how to change the loudness of the sound made by a drum or other musical instrument?

✔ explain how to change the pitch of the sound made by a guitar or other musical instrument?

✔ say what unit of measure is used for sound?

1 Which circuit is a complete circuit so that the lamp will light up?

a    b    c

(1)

2 Look at the two switches.
   a Which switch is on? Which switch is off?
   b Explain how you know this.

   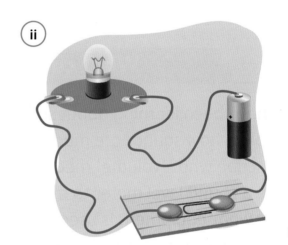

(4)

3 What is wrong with each circuit?

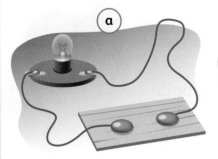   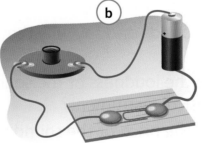   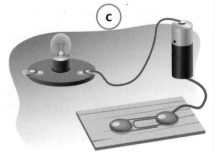

(3)

4 Write True or False for each statement.
  a A magnet is made from metal.
  b Magnets have a magnetic force field.
  c Magnets will attract all materials.
  d Magnetic fields are invisible we cannot see them.   (4)

5 Copy and complete this sentence using two of the words below:
  Magnets attract objects that are made from _____ and
  _____.

(gold)   (nickel)   (silver)   (iron)   (2)

6 Magnets have north and south poles. When the poles of magnets are put
  together, what happens? Write 'attract' or 'repel' for each example.

  a | S   N | N   S |

  b | N   S | S   N |

  c | S   N | S   N |

  d | N   S | N   S | (4)

7 Which of these objects will a magnet attract?
  a plastic ruler
  b iron nail
  c steel screw
  d gold chain   (2)

8 Sounds are made when objects vibrate. What vibrates in each musical instrument to make the sound?

a

b

(2)

9 Jasmine was playing the drum. She found out how to make the volume louder and softer. Copy and complete the sentence that she wrote. Use these words:

(smaller) (vibration) (gently) (harder)

a To change the volume of the sound of the drum you must hit the drum _____ to make a bigger _____ to make a loud sound.

b To make a softer sound you must hit the drum _____ to make _____ vibrations.

(4)

10 Lenny carried out an activity. He found out how sound reaches the ear. Copy and complete the sentence below using these words:

(travelled) (sound) (brain) (hear) (vibrated) (ear)

I put the string in my ear. Then I hit the coat hanger on my table. The coat hanger _____ and the vibration _____ through the string to my _____. My _____ made sense of the _____ that I could _____.

(6)

11 Class 4 measured sound around their school. Here are the results.

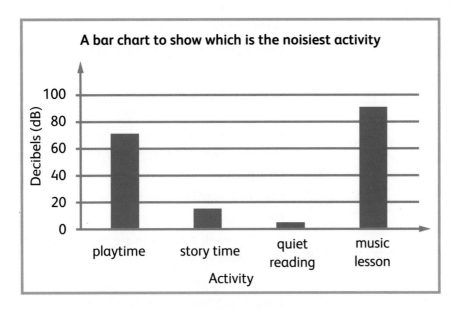

A bar chart to show which is the noisiest activity

Use the bar chart to answer these questions.

a Which is the quietest activity? How do you know?

b How many decibels was the loudest activity?

c Which activity measured 15 dB?

d Put the activities in order, from loudest to softest. (4)

12 Jose blows into bottles that are partly filled with water. The bottles make a sound.

a What is vibrating to make the sound? Is it the air or the water? (1)

b Jose has worked out how to change the pitch. Copy and complete the sentences below using these words:

| column | high-pitched | shorter |

To make a low sound, make the _____ of air in the bottle longer.

To make a _____ sound, make the column of air in the bottle _____. (3)

Total marks: 40

Scientific dictionary

A

Air particles Tiny particles of the gas, air, which we cannot see

Alive To be living

Aluminium A light silvery-grey metal

Annotate To add notes to explain or comment on something

Attract (attracted) To pull towards (a magnet pulls some metal objects towards it)

B

backbone

Backbone Spine or vertebral column

Ball-and-socket joint Allows the body to move bones in different directions

Bar chart A type of graph that uses bars to show results

Bar magnet A magnet in the shape of a bar

Battery Two or more cells that are placed inside a machine (such as a torch) to supply it with electricity so that it works

upper arm (biceps)

Biceps A muscle in the arm that attaches at two points (for example, the large muscle in your upper arm)

Billion One thousand million – a very large number

Blood cells Cells that circulate, or travel around, the blood

Bone marrow The soft material in the middle of bones

Bones Very hard material that forms the skeleton in humans and other vertebrates

Buzzer Something that makes a buzzing sound when it is placed in a circuit

C

Cables Wires with a thick protective casing (for transmitting electricity)

Calcium A mineral found in the hard parts of bones – we need it to build strong bones

Carnivores Meat eaters

Cast A plaster shell to keep a broken bone from moving, or for making a mould

Cells A cell pushes the electric current around the circuit – two cells together are called a battery

Change of state A change from one state of matter to another state of matter (such as solid to liquid)

Circuit Electricity can flow in a complete electric circuit

Circuit break A break in a circuit, which stops the movement of electricity

Circuit components Things such as wires, lamps, buzzers or cells (batteries) that are part of a circuit

Classify (classified) To arrange (arranged) in classes or groups that share features or properties

Column of air In music, air in a cylinder, which can create different sounds

Complete circuit A circuit where the electricity flows all the way around and makes a lamp, buzzer or motor work (such as in an electrical appliance or device)

Components Things or parts that make up a whole thing (such as a circuit)

Conclusion The answer to your question, summing up what you have found out

Condense (condensing) When something changes from a gas or water vapour to a liquid, specifically when it cools

Consistency The way something stays together such as thickness or density

Contaminated Dirtied by waste or pollution – not pure

Contracts Decreases in size – gets smaller

Copper A reddish-brown metal, often used to make low-value coins and wire in electrical circuits

D

Data Information

Data logger Electronic device that can be used to record data over time, for example, sound, light, temperature

Deafness (deaf) Unable to hear

Decibels (dB) Decibels are used to measure the loudness of a sound

Differences Things that are not the same

Drugs Medicine or other substance that affects the mind or body

Dull Not bright or shiny, pale, non-reflective

E

Ear The organ that we use to hear sound

Ear defenders Protection for ears from loud noises

Electrical appliances Devices or items that use electricity to work

Electric current Flow of electricity

Electricity The flow of particles around a circuit

Electric shock Electric current that runs through the body and can be very dangerous

Electromagnet An electromagnet is a piece of metal that becomes magnetic when electricity passes through it or around it

Equipment Things you need to carry out a test

Exoskeleton A hard covering forming the body of some invertebrates (such as grasshoppers and beetles)

exoskeleton

F

Factors Things, facts or features that help to provide a result

Fair test A way to investigate a scientific question

Flexible Bendable

Flow (flows) When electricity moves around a circuit

Flow of particles The movement of tiny bits of invisible material around a circuit, which makes electricity

Force field An invisible wall of force

Fracture A break in a bone

Function The job something does

G

Gas A substance that has no fixed shape and expands to fill any available space

Grow To get bigger in size, for example, taller or wider

H

Habitat The place where an animal or plant lives

Hear To listen to sounds

Hearing The ability to use your ears to listen to sounds

habitat

Herbivores Plant eaters

High (higher) Sounds with a high pitch (in decibels)

Hinge joint Moves like the hinge on a door – backwards and forwards

I

Identification key Used to identify (find the name of) a plant, animal or material – gives choices that lead the user to the correct name

Identify (identification) To find out what something is, for example, a plant, animal or material

Invertebrates An animal (or animals) without a backbone

Iron A strong silvery-grey metal

Iron filings Very small pieces of iron that look like a grey dust and are attracted to a magnet

Irreversible change A change that cannot be undone, for example, if a log burns you cannot get the log back

J

Joints Where two bones meet

L

Lamp Part of a circuit that lights up when switched on

Lamp holder The part that holds a lamp in place

lamp

Life processes Things that something does, which tell us if the object is alive or not, for example, move, reproduce, grow, need nutrition (food and drink)

Line graph A type of chart that shows information as a series of dots (data points) connected by straight lines

Liquid A substance that takes a container's shape (we can pour it)

Loud Making noise at high decibels

Low (lower) Deep sounds

M

Magnetic A piece of iron or steel that has the ability to attract some metals

Magnetic field The area around a magnet that is affected by the magnetic force of the magnet

Magnetic force Responsible for attracting and repelling objects

Magnetic pole Each of the two points of magnetic force of a magnet – north and south

Mains electricity Electric current that flows from a general-purpose supply

Manufacturers Companies with people or machines to make things

Materials Substances that can be used to make something else (for example, wool, leather, concrete)

Matter Everything around us, including ourselves

Medicine A substance (such as a tablet, ointment or syrup) given to a patient to treat illness

Metal A solid material with many properties (such as hard, shiny)

Mind map A chart that helps you to organise your ideas or show what you know

Model (models) A copy of something made out of different materials, for example, a model skeleton – to make something easier to understand

Motor A machine that can make something move

Move To go in a certain direction – in motion

Muscles Soft tissue that stretches across bones and help them to move

N

Nickel A silvery-white metal

Non-magnetic Not magnetic – has no magnetic properties or forces of attraction

North pole The point on the surface of the Northern Hemisphere, where Earth's magnetic field points straight down

Not alive Dead or not living – does not show any of the life processes

Nutrition The food we eat to stay healthy

O

Oil spill A place where oil has leaked into the environment (such as into the sea, a river or a field)

Oil tanker A method of transport for carrying liquids such as oils in huge amounts

Omnivores Eating plants and meat

Opaque A material you cannot see through

Oxygen A colourless, odourless gas that is in the air that we breathe

P

Pharmacy A place to buy medicines

Pitch How high or low a sound is

Poison A substance that can cause humans and animals to be ill or die

Pollution Something that ruins the environment, for example, an oil spill, smoke, car fumes

pollution

Power station A place that generates (makes) electrical power for homes and businesses to use

Predator An animal that catches and eats another animal

Prescription A message written by a doctor for a pharmacist, who packages medicine with instructions on how to use it

Prey An animal that is hunted and eaten by another animal (predator)

Properties How a material looks or behaves

R

Record To write notes for later use

Relax (relaxes) In muscles, to return to its original size, not contracted

Repel To push/force something away

Reproduce When living things make copies of themselves (such as animals have babies, plants make new plants)

Reversible change A change that can be undone, for example, freezing water

Rigid Cannot be moved or bent, not flexible

S

Saliva Spit, watery liquid in mouth, helps us to chew and swallow food

Series circuit Like a circle, each component follows, one after the other (similar to a TV series, where one programme follows the other)

Shelter Something that protects humans and animals from the weather

Shiny Bright, reflective

Sight One of the five senses – being able to use the eyes to see

Silver A precious shiny metal

Similarity (similarities) A thing or things that are nearly the same

Skeleton Bones on the inside of the body, which are joined together to support the body of humans and of other animals

Smell One of the senses, the ability to use the nose to sense (notice) different odours (smells)

Soft Quiet, easy to cut, not hard

Solid A material that has no spaces or gaps and cannot be changed easily – not liquid or gas

Sound A vibration that travels through solids, liquids or gas and can be heard

Solidified When something changes state such as when a liquid turns to ice (goes hard, freezes)

Sound level meter Used to measure the volume of sound

Sources Where something comes from, its origin

Sources of light Things that make light (such as the Sun)

Sources of sound Things that vibrate and make sounds

South pole The point on the surface of the Earth, where Earth's magnetic field points straight up

Spin Turn or twirl around over and over again on the same point

Spindle The small rod on a motor that spins around

Spongy bone Area where the bone grows, has a honeycomb appearance

Standard measurements Used to measure weight, length, capacity and temperature – they are used across the world

States of matter One of the forms of matter (such as solid, liquid, gas)

Steam A mist of water droplets in the air, formed when water boils

Stirrup (stapes) Bone in the ear, shaped liked a stirrup on a horse's saddle, the stapes is the smallest bone in the body

Switch Part of an electrical circuit that stops or allows electricity to flow by opening or closing a gap

Symptoms Physical or mental signs that tell a doctor why you might be ill

T

Taste One of the five senses, the ability to use the tongue to identify different flavours

Tendons A flexible band of tissue that attaches muscle to bone

Termites An insect that often feeds on wood

Thigh bone (femur) The large bone in your upper leg

Touch One of the five senses, the ability to use the skin to feel things and detect different textures

Translucent A material that lets some light through but you cannot see clearly through it

Transparent A material that lets light through and you can see clearly through it

Triceps Muscles attached at three points (at the back of the upper arm, or biceps)

tricep

V

Variable The thing to change when you do a fair test

Venn diagram Represents sets or groups of things in a picture using two circles that overlap

Vertebrates Animals that have a backbone

Vibrate (vibration) When something moves back and forwards, from side to side or up and down quickly

Viscosity A measure of the resistance to flow of a fluid (liquid) – how quickly or slowly a liquid flows

Vitamin D A group of vitamins that we can get from certain foods (and sunlight) – we need vitamin D to be able to absorb calcium

Voice box A hollow tube connected to the windpipe, with two bands of tissue called vocal cords – air passing through the cords makes them vibrate, forming the sound of your voice

Volts The amount of push that a cell gives

Volume The loudness of a sound

W

Waterproof A material that does not let water through

Water vapour The gas between the spout of a kettle and the steam – water vapour is invisible

Wind instrument Musical instrument that someone needs to blow to produce sound

Wire Metal made into a thin flexible cord or thread

X

X-ray A special picture of the bones inside a human or animal

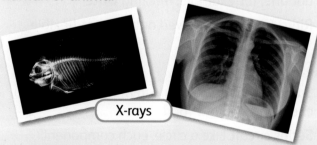

X-rays